The World Turned Upside Down
The American Revolution

Grades 4–5

Center for Gifted Education
School of Education
The College of William and Mary

W&M
Center for
Gifted
Education

Project Director: Joyce VanTassel-Baska, Ed.D.
Project Manager: Linda D. Avery, Ph.D.
Curriculum Coordinator: Catherine A. Little, Ph.D.
Unit Developers: Jeanne M. Struck, Ph.D., Catherine A. Little
Unit Reviewers/Contributors: Dr. Gail McEachron, Dr. Donna Ford,
Dr. Christine L. Hill, Marilyn G. Day

Funded by the Jacob K. Javits Program, United States Department of Education

KENDALL/HUNT PUBLISHING COMPANY
4050 Westmark Drive   Dubuque, Iowa 52002

Book Team

Chairman and Chief Executive Officer: Mark C. Falb
Vice President, Director of National Book Program: Alfred C. Grisanti
Editorial Development Supervisor: Georgia Botsford
Developmental Editor: Angela Willenbring
Prepress Project Coordinator: Sheri Hosek
Prepress Editor: Jenifer Chapman
Permissions Editor: Colleen Zelinsky
Design Manager: Jodi Splinter

Author Information for Correspondence and Workshops:

Center for Gifted Education
The College of William and Mary
P.O. Box 8795
Williamsburg, VA 23187-8795
Phone: 757-221-2362
Email address: cfge@wm.edu
Web address: www.cfge.wm.edu

Cover image © Bettmann/CORBIS

Printed in the United States of America
10 9 8 7 6 5 4

# Contents

Introduction

Part I

Unit Introduction

This social studies unit focuses on the pivotal period in American history leading to and including the American Revolutionary War. The unit is designed around the concept of cause and effect, with emphasis on the idea that history is not inevitable, but is, rather, defined by a series of events and circumstances that affect one another's outcomes. Primary sources and historical summaries are used to explore various perspectives on events of the Revolutionary period and to encourage students in exploring the complexity of history. Students examine the lives of individuals, both famous and ordinary, as they grow to understand what life was like in the early days of our country's history. The activities in the unit will provide opportunity for critical thinking, reasoning, evaluation of reasoning/arguments, and creative thinking. Students will have the opportunity to glean content information about the Revolutionary War from multiple sources, including primary and secondary documents and historical fiction. The combination of activities provided will allow students to view this period in history from multiple viewpoints, providing opportunity for growth in understanding of past events.

Rationale

A social studies curriculum should be an opportunity for students to advance their understanding of several of the individual social science disciplines, as well as the interactions of these disciplines in the real world. In addition, the curriculum should challenge students to think critically and creatively and to recognize connections between their own cultural environment and other cultures in the past and the present. This unit provides such opportunities for students through an interdisciplinary study of the Revolutionary War period in American history.

Curriculum Framework

Concept Goal and Outcomes

Goal 1: To develop understanding of the concept of cause and effect and its relationship to events and eras in history.

Students will be able to . . .

1. Analyze historical situations for cause and effect relationships.

2. Evaluate the degree of influence various causes have upon specific effects.

3. Recognize and explain that the events of history are not inevitable but are related to chains of cause and effect relationships.

4. Identify short- and long-term effects of given causes.

5. Evaluate the degree to which effects are attributable to known causes.

Process Goals and Outcomes

Goal 2: To develop reasoning skills with application to social studies.

Students will be able to . . .

1. State a purpose for all modes of communication—their own as well as those of others.

2. Define a problem, given ill-structured, complex, or technical information.

3. Formulate multiple perspectives (at least two) on a given issue.

4. State assumptions behind a line of reasoning.

5. Apply social studies concepts appropriately.

6. Provide evidence and data to support a claim, issue, or thesis statement.

7. Make inferences based on evidence.

8. Draw implications for policy development or enactment based on the available data.

Goal 3: To develop interpersonal and social group process skills.

Students will be able to . . .

1. Develop a sense of responsibility for creating community.

2. Analyze similarities and differences among the cultural groups studied.

3. Demonstrate personal strategies for managing and resolving conflicts in groups.

4. Utilize appropriate problem-solving strategies, given a group problem.

Goal 4: To develop skills in historical analysis and primary source interpretation.

Students will be able to . . .

1. Define the context in which a primary source document was produced, as well as the implications of context for understanding the document.

2. Describe an author's intent in producing a given document based on understanding of text and context.

3. Analyze a document to define problem, argument, assumptions, and expected outcomes.

4. Evaluate the influence of author and audience bias in a given document.

5. Validate a source as to its authenticity, authority, and representativeness.

6. Research short- and long-term consequences of a given document.

7. Analyze effects of given sources on interpretation of historical events.

Content Goal and Outcomes

Goal 5: To develop understanding of the causes of the American Revolution, the major events and influential individuals of the period, and the reasons for the American victory.

Students will be able to . . .

1. Analyze the causes and circumstances surrounding the growing hostility between the American colonies and Great Britain in the period 1763–1775.

2. Trace the chronology of critical events of the American Revolution and the influences of them on the outcomes.

3. Analyze key documents of the period, including the Stamp Act and Stamp Act Resolutions, the Declaration of Independence, and Common Sense.

4. Use historical fiction and contemporary accounts to explore portrayals of life in the Revolutionary period for various groups of affected individuals.

5. Identify and explicate the influence of key figures of the Revolutionary period.

6. Discuss the implications of the Revolution for the next steps of the new nation.

Dear Teacher:

The unit you are about to begin, *The World Turned Upside Down: The American Revolution,* consists of 20 lessons, each designed to take from one to two hours of instruction. Following this letter is a letter for parents that you may wish to send home with your students or use as a template for your own letter home. The letter describes the goals of the curriculum, as well as ways parents can supplement the unit at home.

The unit includes many opportunities for independent and group activities for students. Some of these activities involve homework as well as classwork, and some also involve research to be conducted in a library/media center or on-line. Please read through the unit before beginning to get a sense of when you might need materials or assistance from your media specialist and to inform parents of upcoming assignments at home.

All of the handouts and many of the student readings for the unit are included, and a materials list at the start of each lesson will tell you specific items needed for that lesson. However, there are a few additional items you may wish to procure before beginning the unit:

- ◆ Copies for students of several historical fiction pieces set in the Revolutionary period. You may wish to select one novel for the whole class to read or (as suggested in the lesson plans) have groups reading different novels. Suggested titles are *The Fighting Ground* by Avi, *My Brother Sam is Dead* by James and Christopher Collier, and *Sarah Bishop* by Scott O'Dell.

- ◆ Resource materials on the Revolutionary period, including primary and secondary source readings, recordings of music, art prints, and artifacts if possible (some suggestions are listed in the resources section at the end of the unit).

- ◆ Text: Most of the readings of this unit are primary source readings from the Revolutionary period and brief secondary pieces focused on particular events. You may wish to have American history textbooks on hand for students to read "big picture summaries" of the events as well, although the emphasis should be on the primary sources as given in the handouts.

- ◆ Bookmarks: Extensive resources on the Revolutionary period are available on the Internet. You may wish to preview and bookmark a few selected sites for students to explore during the unit. Some suggested sites are listed in the resources section at the end of the unit.

The Center for Gifted Education thanks you for your interest in our materials!

Dear Parents,

Your child is involved in a special social studies unit called *The World Turned Upside Down: The American Revolution.* We will be studying the Revolutionary period in American history and learning about the causes and effects of the various events that occurred. The main goals of the unit are listed below.

Goal 1: To develop understanding of the concept of cause and effect and its relationship to events and eras in history

Goal 2: To develop reasoning skills with application to social studies

Goal 3: To develop inter-personal and social group process skills

Goal 4: To develop skills in historical analysis and primary source interpretation

Goal 5: To develop understanding of the causes of the American Revolution, the major events and influential individuals of the period, and the reasons for the American victory

To help us meet these goals, we will be examining maps, documents, and other resources. We will discuss the ideas we discover in class and complete several projects to demonstrate new understanding. Students will be required to participate in both critical and creative writing activities, group research projects, and independent reading of historical fiction and non-fiction literature. The students will keep a journal during the unit to respond to reflective questions about the time period and the implications of the events and ideas discussed. We will discuss our findings and insights as a class as we progress through the unit. The students will be challenged to think critically about the information they encounter.

This unit includes several activities which will require some work outside of class. Your child may need your support at home on the following activities:

1. Independent reading that includes a novel set during the Revolution and other selected documents and resources

2. Written homework assignments

3. Research project on a prominent individual during the period

4. Group research project on regional military events

Independent work will be discussed in class, and further information will be sent home as assignments are given. There will be opportunities for students to work with the teacher and classmates on each project as the unit progresses.

Student progress in the unit will be assessed in several ways. First, pre-tests will be used to assess skill and knowledge in the unit content, process, and concepts. Secondly, students will keep a unit journal and a portfolio for their writing and other activities. Finally, post-tests will be used to compare student achievement at the end of the unit to their work at the beginning. I also welcome comments from parents on how the unit is progressing.

Good curriculum and instructional practice should involve parents as well as teachers. The following ideas may be useful as your child experiences the unit:

- Read the materials your child is reading and discuss main ideas.
- Hold a family debate on one of the issues discussed in the unit.
- Encourage your child to write every day in a diary or journal.
- When watching movies or TV together, discuss the ideas presented with your child, and encourage close attention to how ideas are handled in the media.
- Watch the news and/or read the newspaper with your child; discuss current events and relate these events to events from history.
- Look at maps and globes together to find the places we talk about in class.
- Visit the library, a museum, or a local historic site to find out more about unit topics.

Thank you in advance for your interest in your child's curriculum. Please do not hesitate to contact me for further information as the unit progresses.

Sincerely,

Unit Glossary

allegiance—loyalty to a nation or cause

alliance—an association of nations united in a common cause or interest; or a formal agreement establishing such an association

assumption—something that is taken for granted or accepted as true without proof

authenticity—the condition of being trustworthy or genuine or of having verifiable origin

camp follower—a civilian who follows a unit of the military from place to place

capitulation—the act of giving up or surrendering, usually under specified conditions

cause—the person, thing, event, or condition that is responsible for an action, result, or effect; also a goal or principle served with dedication

cease-fire—a truce; a suspension or stopping of hostilities

chronology—the arrangement or sequence of events in time

coincidence—a set or sequence of events that seem to be related or planned but are actually accidental in relationship to one another

commander-in-chief—the supreme commander of a nation's armed forces

confederation—a group of states or nations united for a common purpose

congress—a formal assembly of representatives, usually for discussion of a specific problem or issue; or the legislative body of a nation

constitution—the system of laws or principles that prescribes the nature, functions, and limits of a government

correlation—a relationship that is parallel or complementary, in that two or more conditions occur together or in a related way, but in which one of the conditions does not necessarily cause the other

coup—the sudden overthrow of a government

debt—something that is owed, such as money, goods, or services, or the condition of owing *declaration*—a formal announcement or statement, either written or oral

diplomacy—the practice of conducting international relations, such as developing alliances and treaties among governments

drills—training of soldiers in tasks such as marching and using weapons

duty—a tax charged by a government, usually related to tax on imports

effect—something that happens or occurs as a result of a cause

evidence—data or information helpful in forming an inference, conclusion, or judgment

flag—a piece of cloth of specific color and design, used as a symbol or emblem

grievance—a complaint or protest; or a circumstance seen as just cause for complaint or protest

hindsight—an understanding of events and their importance gained after the events have occurred

historical fiction—a literary work that recreates a period or event in history, often using both fictional and actual characters

homefront—the context and activities of civilians in a country at war

huzza—a shout or loud cry, used to express joy or triumph

implication—a suggestion of likely or logical consequence; a logical relationship between two linked propositions or statements

independence—for a country, the condition of being free and self-governing, not governed by a foreign power

inference—a conclusion drawn from factual knowledge or evidence; the act of reasoning or thinking through questions to derive logical conclusions based on what is known

intolerable—unbearable, impossible to endure or accept

liberty—freedom from restriction or control; the right to act, believe, and express oneself according to one's own choosing

Loyalist—an American colonist who favored the British side during the Revolution; also called Tory

massacre—the killing of a large number of people, usually very cruelly and with helpless or unresisting victims

militia—an army of ordinary citizens, not professional soldiers; organized armed forces called on only in emergency

morale—the spirits of a person or group; the level of cheerfulness, confidence, and willingness to work

musket—a large, heavy shoulder gun widely used in the 16th through 18th centuries

officer—a person in a position of authority or command in the armed forces

olive branch—an offer of peace or goodwill, based on traditional symbolism of the branch of the olive tree representing peace

Parliament—the legislature of the United Kingdom, including the House of Lords and House of Commons, which maintained law-making power over British colonies

parody—a literary, artistic, or musical work that imitates the style of another work or author for ridicule or comic effect

patriot—one who loves, defends, or protects his or her country and supports its authority

Patriot—term used to refer to those who supported the American colonial cause against the British government during the Revolutionary period

persuasive writing—a form of writing designed to convince the reader of the author's point of view on an issue

petition—a formal document making a request of a person or group in authority; often requesting a right or benefit

philosopher—a scholar whose focus is inquiry into reality through logical reasoning; one who strives to achieve and share wisdom

point of view—an attitude, opinion, or position from which a person understands a situation or issue

predictable—something that can be known in advance to be about to happen; can also describe expected behaviors

present-mindedness—the application of current values and ideals to events and contexts of the past, without consideration of the values and ideals influencing those events at the time of their occurrence

primary source—a document or other product created by someone who was present at the event or time being written about

propaganda—the deliberate spreading of ideas, information, or rumor to support a cause or damage an opposing cause

quartering—providing housing, especially for military troops

radical—favoring major or revolutionary changes in current practices, conditions, or institutions

reasoning—thinking to form conclusions, inferences, or judgments about an issue

Rebel—a person involved in a rebellion or resistance against an established government; term used by the British to refer to the Patriots during the Revolution

repeal—to revoke or cancel a law or act through another official act

representation—the condition of serving as an official delegate or spokesperson of the interests of a group, especially to a legislative body

representative—similar to or typical of others of the same class or group

resignation—the formal act of giving up a position or office

resolution—a formal statement of a decision, point of view, or intent of an official assembly or group

revolution—the overthrow of a government to replace it with another; a momentous change in a situation or cultural context

riot—a violent disturbance of the public peace by a group of people

secondary source—a document or product created by a person who was not present at the event or time being written about but is using other people's accounts and other records of an event to write about it

self-evident—requiring no proof, explanation, or reasoning

siege—a military blockade of a city or fortress in order to force it to surrender

stakeholder—a person who has an interest in or involvement with an enterprise or issue and its potential outcomes

Stamp Act—1765 law passed in Parliament to gain funds through taxes levied on paper products in the colonies

state—the political organization of a group of people usually occupying a given territory; may be a sovereign government or one of a group that together form a nation with a federal government

subject—a person who is under the rule or authority of another, especially referring to the rule or authority of a government or ruler

surrender—to give oneself up or to relinquish control, as to an enemy

symbol—something that represents another thing, especially a concrete object used to represent something abstract

tax—a contribution to support a government required of those persons and groups under that government's domain

thruppence—a sum of money, abbreviated form of three pence or three pennies

Tory—an American colonist loyal to the British cause during the Revolution; also called Loyalist *tread*—to walk on or over, to trample

treatise—a systematic argument in writing on a subject, usually an extensive document

tyranny—absolute power in a government; actions demonstrating absolute power, especially unjust or cruel actions

unalienable—describing things not to be separated or taken away

unanimous—having the complete agreement of all members of a group

union—(on a flag) a device or design, usually in the upper inner corner of a flag, representing the union or joining of two or more sovereign groups

unpredictable—something that cannot be known in advance to be about to happen; can also describe unexpected behaviors

Yankee—term used by British soldiers in the colonial period to ridicule New Englanders, adopted popularly by New Englanders to describe themselves after the battle of Lexington; the term has been used to describe all Americans but also to describe specifically Northerners

Lesson Plans

Part II

Introduction to Unit and Pre-Assessment

Lesson 1

Curriculum Alignment

Goal 1	Goal 2	Goal 3	Goal 4	Goal 5
X	X		X	X

 Instructional Purpose

- ◆ To introduce students to the topics of the unit
- ◆ To assess student knowledge and understanding of unit topics
- ◆ To use primary source material to infer information about events
- ◆ To develop questions of interest about a topic

 Materials

1. American Revolution Pre-Assessment (Handout 1A)
2. American Revolution Assessment Scoring Guide (Teacher Resource 1)
3. *The Rich Lady over the Sea* (Handout 1B)
4. Chart paper

 Vocabulary

evidence—data or information helpful in forming an inference, conclusion, or judgment

inference—a conclusion drawn from factual knowledge or evidence; the act of reasoning or thinking through questions to derive logical conclusions based on what is known

reasoning—thinking to form conclusions, inferences, or judgments about an issue

revolution—the overthrow of a government to replace it with another; a momentous change in a situation or cultural context

thruppence—a sum of money, abbreviated form of three pence or three pennies

📖 Activities

1. Explain to students that they will be beginning a unit about the American Revolution which will help them to learn about why the Revolution happened, what the major events were, who the important people were, and what life was like during that time period. Tell students that in order to help you get a sense of what they already know and to provide a basis for comparison of what they have learned by the end, they will be taking a pre-test. Distribute the **American Revolution Pre-Assessment** (Handout 1A) and have students complete. Collect the pre-assessments.

2. Have students take a few minutes independently to write down a list of details they already know about the Revolution and a list of questions they have about this period in American history. Have students share their ideas, and create a class list on chart paper to post in the classroom during the unit.

3. Distribute copies of *The Rich Lady over the Sea* (Handout 1B). Tell students this is the text of a song that was sung in the 1770s in America. Ask students to read the words of the song silently and to write for a few minutes explaining what they think the song is about and why. Invite students to share their ideas. Tell students that the song is a metaphor for the relationship between England and the American colonies in the early 1770s, before the beginning of the American Revolution that led to the establishment of the United States as an independent nation. Ask students if knowing that information changes how they think about the song.

4. Tell students that while they learn about the Revolution in this unit, they will also be learning a way of thinking about problems, issues, or questions that will help them think not only about school issues, but about other issues as well. Explain that as they work through the unit, they will be learning eight Elements of Reasoning and how to use the different elements.

5. Introduce the term *inference* to students. Tell students that inferences are little conclusions or understandings that we draw about problems, issues, or questions based on *evidence or data*. These two elements of reasoning—inferences and evidence—are very important because they help us to use facts and details to make decisions instead of "jumping to conclusions." For example, if we are shopping for a new pair of sneakers, we might explore evidence about prices and

quality of different brands before making our decision, instead of relying only on what advertisements say. Tell students that you are now going to ask them to use the song lyrics they read to make some inferences about the time of the Revolution. Ask students to respond briefly in writing to the following questions and then discuss:

- *Why do you think the person who wrote this song chose to compare Britain and the American colonies to a mother and daughter? What inferences can you make about the relationship between Britain and America based on that comparison?*

- *What specific details in the song tell you how the person writing it felt about Britain at the time?*

- *Is the song making fun of anyone or anything? How do you know?*

6. Tell students that as they work through the unit, they will be learning much more about the elements of reasoning.

Journal

How do you think your reading of the song *The Rich Lady over the Sea* might be different from that of someone who read it in the 1770s? How does your understanding of what eventually happened affect the way you read the song?

Homework

Choose a book and pick three pages at random. Read the three pages and count how many times the word "because" is used. Look carefully at each of the uses, and see if you can identify a *cause and effect* relationship that the sentence is talking about. Then write a response to this question: What do we mean when we say *cause and effect*?

Extension

Expand the focus of the unit by having students "explore the world" in 1765. Assign groups of students different regions or countries of the world, and have them find out (1) the type of government in the region in 1765 and today and (2) the political borders in the region in 1765 and today.

Notes to Teacher

1. Please send home the letter to parents with each student who is engaged in the unit.

2. The pre-assessment given in this lesson serves multiple purposes. Performance on the pre-assessment should establish a baseline against which performance on the post-assessment may be compared. In addition, teachers may use information obtained from pre-assessments to aid instructional planning as strengths and areas for improvement among students become apparent.

3. Including the pre-assessment, this lesson may take more than one class period to complete.

4. Students should have a unit notebook or folder that they can use throughout the unit to respond to journal questions and other written assignments and to keep any handouts from the unit. The folder can also hold a running list of unit vocabulary, which can additionally be displayed in the classroom in chart form.

5. The model for reasoning introduced briefly here will be used in much greater detail throughout the unit. All of the elements are explained more fully in the implementation section. This unit serves as a companion to the unit *Building a New System: Colonial America 1607–1763*. If both units are to be used, students will already have some familiarity with the reasoning elements, but will still require guidance and practice with using them.

6. If possible, share a recording of the song in this lesson with students as well as the text. In addition, you may wish to set up a classroom center as an audio station for listening to songs from the Revolutionary period and responding to them in writing or discussion. One source for music of the Revolution is Keith and Rusty McNeil's *Colonial and Revolution Songs* from WEM Records and the accompanying *Colonial and Revolution Songbook*. Several additional sources are listed in the resources section of the unit.

Assessment

- ◆ Journal responses
- ◆ Responses/participation in discussion
- ◆ Responses to pre-assessment

American Revolution
Pre-Assessment

Circle the BEST response to each question.

1. Which of these was NOT a reason why Congress chose George Washington to be commander in chief of the Continental Army?
    a. Washington applied for the job.
    b. Washington was not from New England.
    c. Washington had experience in the army.
    d. Washington was the only candidate seriously considered for the job.

2. What was the main reason for the colonial opposition to the Stamp Act?
    a. Taxes under the Stamp Act would put a large financial burden on the colonists.
    b. The Stamp Act was the first major tax imposed by Great Britain on the colonies.
    c. The Stamp Act emphasized to colonists that they did not have a voice in Parliament.
    d. Taxes collected under the Stamp Act would not provide any benefits for the colonies.

3. Which of the following statements was NOT one of the purposes of the Declaration of Independence?
    a. To identify the actions of the king that the colonists felt were unjust
    b. To apply a philosophy about people's natural rights to the colonial situation
    c. To outline details for a new system of government for the colonies
    d. To show official commitment to the Revolutionary movement

4. Which of the following was the most important factor influencing the start of the fighting in the Revolution?
    a. Tensions stirred up in New England by radical colonists opposing British actions
    b. British movement of troops into the major ports of New York, Philadelphia, and Charleston
    c. The Continental Congress's decision to declare independence from Great Britain
    d. Thomas Paine's pamphlet *Common Sense* saying the colonies should be free from Britain

5. Which of these statements is true about African American participation in the Revolutionary War?
   a. African Americans were not allowed to fight in the Continental Army because Southern leaders were afraid of slave revolts.
   b. British military leaders promised African American slaves their freedom if they ran away from their masters to fight for the king.
   c. All African Americans in this period were slaves, so they could only fight if their masters sent them to the army or if they ran away.
   d. Most African Americans supported the British because they believed the British could offer them a better life in the West Indies.

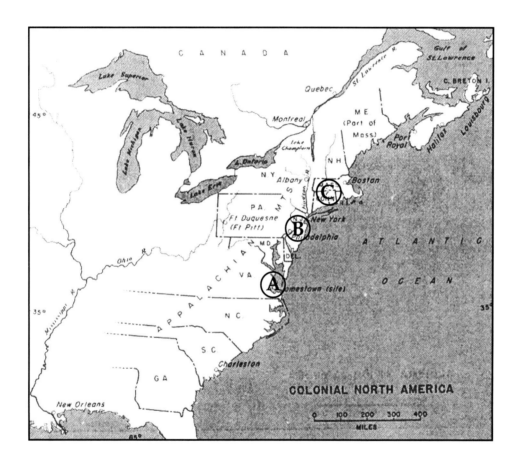

6. Look at the map. Which set of letters shows the order in which most of the fighting progressed?
   a. ABC
   b. BCA
   c. CAB
   d. CBA

7. Which of the following factors contributed MOST to the American victory in the War for Independence?

    a. Support for the war from the majority of the American people

    b. Major American victories in battle at Bunker Hill, Saratoga, and Valley Forge

    c. Financial and military support for the Americans from France

    d. Military superiority of the American troops

8. Which of these statements is the best explanation of this description of governments from the Declaration of Independence: "deriving their just powers from the consent of the governed"?

    a. The purpose of a government is to pass laws and to make sure that the laws are followed.

    b. Government has authority over people because the people agree to give authority to the government.

    c. People have unalienable rights to life, liberty, and property, and governments must protect those rights.

    d. The king of England was unjust to the colonists, so he should not have governmental power.

9. Which of these pairs of statements shows an accurate cause and effect relationship?

    a. George Washington was appointed commander in chief of the army, so the American troops drove the British from Lexington and Concord back to Boston.

    b. Five colonists were killed in the Boston Massacre, so the Sons of Liberty dumped the British tea into the harbor in the Boston Tea Party.

    c. The Continental Congress voted to accept the Virginia Resolutions, so Thomas Jefferson wrote the Declaration of Independence.

    d. The Continental Army showed its ability to win at Saratoga, so the French government signed a treaty of alliance with the United States.

10. Put the following events into the order in which they happened. Place a **1** beside the earliest event, a **2** beside the second event, and so on.

    _____ The Boston Tea Party

    _____ The Battle of Bunker Hill

    _____ The Battle of Saratoga

    _____ The signing of the Declaration of Independence

    _____ The Tea Act

Write your responses to each of the questions below.

11. Choose one of these acts of Parliament. Explain what the act said, why Parliament passed it, and what some of its effects were.
    - The Stamp Act
    - The Tea Act
    - The Quartering Act

    _____

    _____

    _____

    _____

    _____

    _____

12. Select two of the following individuals. For each one, explain who the person was and why he or she was important in the Revolutionary period.
    - Thomas Paine
    - Abigail Adams
    - Benjamin Franklin
    - Lord Cornwallis

    _____

    _____

    _____

    _____

    _____

13. List and explain two causes of the American Revolution.

_____

_____

_____

_____

_____

14. Describe two different roles that women played during the Revolutionary War. For each role, explain how it was a change for women from their lives before the war.

_____

_____

_____

_____

_____

Read the excerpt below, from a speech given by Patrick Henry to the Virginia Assembly in March of 1775, and answer the questions.

> If we wish to be free ... we must fight! I repeat it, sir, we must fight! They tell us, sir, that we are weak; unable to cope with so formidable an adversary. But when shall we be stronger? Will it be the next week, or the next year? Will it be when we are totally disarmed, and when a British guard shall be stationed in every house? ...
>
> Gentlemen may cry, Peace, Peace—but there is no peace. The war is actually begun! The next gale that sweeps from the north will bring to our ears the clash of resounding arms! Our brethren are already in the field! Why stand we here idle?

What is it that gentlemen wish? What would they have? Is life so dear, or peace so sweet, as to be purchased at the price of chains and slavery? Forbid it, Almighty God! I know not what course others may take; but as for me, give me liberty or give me death!

15. What is the purpose of the speech?

_____

_____

_____

_____

16. Name two implications Patrick Henry suggests of not supporting his point of view.

_____

_____

_____

_____

17. Explain in your own words the statement "Give me liberty or give me death" and how it applied to Patrick Henry's situation.

_____

_____

_____

_____

American Revolution Assessment Scoring Guide

Circle the BEST response to each question.

1. a.
2. c.
3. c.
4. a.
5. b.
6. d.
7. c.
8. b.
9. d.

Scoring for questions 1–9:

Score 2 points for each correct response.

Score 0 points for each incorrect response.

10. Put the following events into the order in which they happened. Place a 1 beside the earliest event, a 2 beside the second event, and so on.

_2_ The Boston Tea Party

_3_ The Battle of Bunker Hill

_5_ The Battle of Saratoga

_4_ The signing of the Declaration of Independence

_1_ The Tea Act

Scoring for question 10:

Score 4 points if all five events are correctly numbered.

Score 2 points if at least three consecutive events are grouped together in the correct order but not all five.

Score 1 point if two consecutive events are grouped together in the correct order.

Score 0 points if none of the above criteria apply.

Write your responses to each of the questions below.

11. Choose one of these Acts of Parliament. Explain what the act said, why Parliament passed it, and what some of its effects were.

    ◆ The Stamp Act

    ◆ The Tea Act

    ◆ The Quartering Act

    Possible responses include *the Stamp Act required colonists to pay for official stamps on many different types of documents, Parliament passed it to help bring in funds to pay for the expenses from the French and Indian War, colonists reacted against it because they felt they had no say in it, colonies came together in Stamp Act Congress and protested it; the Tea Act put a tax on tea for the colonies but allowed the British East India Company to undersell colonial merchants, Parliament hoped to support the East India Company, the colonists protested and boycotted the tea, the Boston Tea Party occurred; the Quartering Act required colonists to quarter British troops or take them into their homes and feed them, Parliament passed it to protect the colonists from hostile Indians but also to keep watch on the colonists and to provide shelter for troops, colonists reacted against it and used it as a basis for protest with other acts.*

    Scoring for question 11:

    *Score **4** points if response identifies an act, its purpose, and at least one clearly related effect.*

    *Score **2** points if response identifies an act and makes an attempt to demonstrate Parliament's purpose and/or a related effect.*

    *Score **0** points if none of the above criteria apply.*

12. Select two of the following individuals. For each one, explain who the person was and why he or she was important in the Revolutionary period.

    ◆ Thomas Paine

    ◆ Abigail Adams

    ◆ Benjamin Franklin

    ◆ Lord Cornwallis

    Possible responses include *Thomas Paine was an Englishman living in the colonies who wrote the pamphlet Common Sense encouraging the colonies to declare independence, his writings were very popular and influenced political decision-making during the Revolution; Abigail Adams was the wife of John Adams,* one of the prominent members of the Continental Congress, her letters to her husband and his letters to her show reactions to major events of the time, she encouraged her husband to remember the importance of rights for women as well as men; Benjamin Franklin was a leading supporter of colonial independence and a member of the committee that prepared the Declaration of Independence, he went to France as a representative of the colonies for much of the war and helped ensure the French-American alliance; Lord Cornwallis was a British Army general who was very successful against the Americans especially in the Southern states toward the end of the war, he was planning to join with forces from New York to strike a major blow to the Continental Army in Virginia but was boxed in by the French and Americans and surrendered at Yorktown, basically ending the war.

Scoring for question 12:

*Score **4** points if response identifies two individuals correctly with at least one key detail for each.*

*Score **2** points if response identifies one individual correctly with at least one key detail.*

*Score **0** points if none of the above criteria apply.*

13. List and explain two causes of the American Revolution.

Possible responses include *colonial opposition to taxation, with colonists protesting taxation without representation and the types of taxes and restrictions passed; public attention to radical colonial groups who promoted ideas of independence and took positions of leadership to further those ideas; tensions between colonists and British troops stationed in the colonies that escalated into violence; economic opportunities for the colonies that would increase without British restrictions on trade; philosophies of government that suggested possibilities for different directions for the colonies.*

Scoring for question 13:

*Score **4** points if response identifies two valid causes of the Revolution AND provides elaboration on why each was an issue.*

*Score **2** points if response identifies two valid causes of the Revolution and provides elaboration on at least one.*

*Score **1** point if response identifies and explains one valid cause.*

*Score **0** points if none of the above criteria apply.*

14. Describe two different roles that women played during the Revolutionary War. For each role, explain how it was a change for women from their lives before the war.

   Possible responses include *taking on work at home formerly done by men; being "camp followers" and traveling with the army to cook, clean, carry water, and help with the sick; fighting in battle in disguise as men; being spies; opening their homes to house troops.*

   Scoring for question 14:

   Score **4** points if response identifies at least two roles and how they caused change.

   Score **2** points if response identifies at two roles but does not provide explanation of change.

   Score **1** point if response identifies one role.

   Score **0** points if none of the above criteria apply.

Read the excerpt below, from a speech given by Patrick Henry to the Virginia Assembly in March of 1775, and answer the questions.

   If we wish to be free … we must fight! I repeat it, sir, we must fight! They tell us, sir, that we are weak; unable to cope with so formidable an adversary. But when shall we be stronger? Will it be the next week, or the next year? Will it be when we are totally disarmed, and when a British guard shall be stationed in every house? …

   Gentlemen may cry, Peace, Peace—but there is no peace. The war is actually begun! The next gale that sweeps from the north will bring to our ears the clash of resounding arms! Our brethren are already in the field! Why stand we here idle? What is it that gentlemen wish? What would they have? Is life so dear, or peace so sweet, as to be purchased at the price of chains and slavery? Forbid it, Almighty God! I know not what course others may take; but as for me, give me liberty or give me death!

15. What is the purpose of the speech? What evidence supports your response?

   Possible responses include *to raise support in the Assembly for the Patriot cause, to encourage a sense of connection with rising tensions in Massachusetts, to predict possibilities for the future if colonists did not act, to convince the Assembly of the seriousness of the situation between the colonies and Britain.*

Scoring for question 15:

Score 4 points if response clearly identifies and supports at least one purpose of the speech.

Score 2 points if response identifies a valid purpose and makes an attempt to support.

Score 0 points if none of the above criteria apply.

16. Name two implications Patrick Henry suggests of not supporting his point of view.

Possible responses include *weapons and ways of defending themselves taken away from the colonies, British troops stationed in every house in the colonies, increased restrictions on life in the colonies.*

Scoring for question 16:

Score 4 points if response clearly identifies two valid implications from the speech.

Score 2 points if response clearly identifies one valid implication from the speech.

Score 0 points if none of the above criteria apply.

17. Explain in your own words the statement "Give me liberty or give me death" and how it applied to Patrick Henry's situation.

Possible responses include *freedom or liberty is the most important thing in life to me, I would rather lose my life than live without freedom, liberty is more important than anything else in life; Patrick Henry believed the situation between the colonies and Great Britain had reached a point of no return, that either the colonists had to fight for their freedom, live in "slavery," or die, he was pledging his life to the cause of liberty for the colonies, he wanted the members of the Virginia Assembly to pledge their lives to the fight.*

Scoring for question 17:

Score 4 points if response explains the words and the context of the quote clearly.

Score 2 points if response explains the words of the quote and attempts to relate it to Henry's situation.

Score 0 points if none of the above criteria apply.

The Rich Lady Over the Sea

Verse 1

There was a rich lady lived over the sea,
And she was an island queen.
Her daughter lived off in the new country,
With an ocean of water between.
With an ocean of water between,
With an ocean of water between.

Verse 2

The old lady's pockets were filled with gold,
Yet never contented was she,
So she ordered her daughter to pay her a tax
Of thruppence a pound on the tea.
Of thruppence a pound on the tea,
Of thruppence a pound on the tea.

Verse 3

"Oh mother, dear mother," the daughter replied,
"I'll not do the thing that you ask,
I'm willing to pay a fair price on the tea,
But never the thruppenney tax.
But never the thruppenney tax,
But never the thruppenney tax."

Verse 4

"You shall!" cried the mother, and reddened with rage,
"For you're my own daughter, you see,
And it's only proper that daughter should pay
Her mother a tax on the tea.
Her mother a tax on the tea,
Her mother a tax on the tea."

Verse 5

She ordered her servant to come up to her,
And to wrap up a package of tea,
And eager for thruppence a pound she put in
Enough for a large family.
Enough for a large family,
Enough for a large family.

Verse 6

The tea was conveyed to her daughter's own door,
All down by the oceanside,
But the bouncing girl poured out every pound
On the dark and the boiling tide.
On the dark and the boiling tide,
On the dark and the boiling tide.

Verse 7

And then she called out to the island queen,
"Oh mother, dear mother," called she,
"Your tea you may have when 'tis steeped enough,
But never a tax from me!
But never a tax from me,
But never a tax from me!"

Source: McNeil and McNeil, *Colonial and Revolution Songbook,* pp. 40–41.

Introduction to Cause and Effect

Curriculum Alignment

Goal 1	Goal 2	Goal 3	Goal 4	Goal 5
X		X		

Instructional Purpose

♦ To develop an understanding of the concept of cause and effect

♦ To apply generalizations about cause and effect to specific examples

Materials

1. Cause and Effect Model (Handout 2A)

2. Sample Cause and Effect Model (Teacher Resource 2)

3. Chart paper

Vocabulary

cause—the person, thing, event, or condition that is responsible for an action, result, or effect; also a goal or principle served with dedication

coincidence—a set or sequence of events that seem to be related or planned but are actually accidental in relationship to one another

correlation—a relationship that is parallel or complementary, in that two or more conditions occur together or in a related way, but in which one of the conditions does not necessarily cause the other

effect—something that happens or occurs as a result of a cause

hindsight—an understanding of events and their importance gained after the events have occurred

predictable—something that can be known in advance to be about to happen; can also describe expected behaviors

unpredictable—something that cannot be known in advance to be about to happen; can also describe unexpected behaviors

📖 Activities

1. Tell students that often when we look at events in history or in our own lives, we try to figure out *why* these events happened and to identify *causes*. We also try to predict the *effects* of our actions. However, most of the time in history cause and effect are pretty complicated, and it is not easy to identify simple causes or effects of events. Explain to students that as they work through this unit, they will be exploring the concept of cause and effect as it relates to the Revolutionary period in American history.

2. Have students share their homework responses from the previous lesson. Ask students to define what is meant by the phrase cause and effect.

   ◆ *What is a cause?*

   ◆ *What is an effect?*

   ◆ *How do you know when two events have a cause and effect relationship?*

   Have students suggest one to two examples of cause-effect relationships.

3. Divide students into small groups. Give each group a large sheet of paper. Ask each group to brainstorm some more examples of cause and effect. Encourage them to think about cause and effect relationships in nature and in people's lives, considering as many different types of relationships as they can. Use questions such as the following to help start students' thinking:

   ◆ *What are some examples of cause and effect?*

   ◆ *What are some cause and effect relationships in nature?*

   ◆ *What are some cause and effect relationships that require the involvement of people?*

   ◆ *How do you know something is an effect of a particular cause?*

   (some examples of simple cause and effect relationships: water a plant ➪ it grows, stays alive; eat too much ➪ get a stomachache; study for a test ➪ do well on the test; scare a cat ➪ get scratched; drop a glass ➪ it breaks)

4. Encourage each group to share some of their examples of cause and effect relationships with the class. Then have

students return to their groups and figure out how they can group their cause-effect relationships into categories. Have them create their categories and then assign each category a name. Use questions such as the following to help students in categorizing their examples:

- *How could you separate these cause-effect relationships into different groups?*

- *What are some things that a few of the examples might have in common?*

- *Once you have put your examples into groups, what would you call each group?*

- *Why did you decide that each group of examples went together?*

- *Do all of your examples fall into groups?*

- *Might some of them belong in more than one group?*

(some potential categories: cause-effect relationships that occur because of natural laws such as gravity; cause-effect relationships that occur because of human-determined rules, such as the consequences of breaking rules; cause-effect relationships that occur because of people's emotional reactions to events or situations; cause-effect relationships over which people can exert control versus those over which people have little or no control; cause-effect relationships that reflect results of an active cause versus those that reflect results of choosing not to act, etc.)

5. Next explain to students that when we are trying to understand what a concept means, it is helpful to come up with not only examples of the concept, but also non-examples. Ask students to think about relationships between events that are non-examples of cause and effect. Have students return to their groups to try to find some non-examples. Use questions such as the following to help students in their thinking:

- *When two events happen that seem to be related to each other somehow, do they always represent a cause-effect relationship?*

- *How can you tell if two events are causally related?*

- *What are some situations that would not be examples of cause-effect relationships?*

- *How could you categorize your non-examples?*

◆ *How do the following ideas relate to the concept of cause and effect: superstitions, coincidences, related characteristics?*

[some potential non-examples: picking up a penny ⇨ something lucky happens, or other superstitions; two students in a class have the same name; interest in sports and athletic achievement, etc. Note that list of non-examples is likely to be much shorter than and more difficult to determine than list of examples; if students are having great difficulty with non-examples, it may be wise to do this portion of the activity as a whole group instead of as a small group.]

6. Invite students to share their non-examples. Discuss the differences between the list of examples and the list of non-examples. Why are the items on the second list not examples of cause and effect? Explain to students that by listing the non-examples as well as the examples, they will gain a stronger understanding of what the concept of cause and effect means.

7. Tell students that the next step in the process is to come up with some generalizations about cause and effect, or statements that can be used to describe things that are always or almost always true about the concept. Explain that generalizations are kind of like definitions but that they go beyond definitions by explaining more about how we understand the concept. Ask students to look back at their lists of examples, categories, and non-examples and to think about the process they went through to try to come up with one or two generalizations about cause and effect. Give students time to work on generalizations in their groups, then encourage them to share their generalizations and discuss.

8. Tell students that in this unit they will focus on six generalizations about cause and effect as they study the American Revolution. Introduce each of the following six generalizations, and use the suggested questions to encourage discussion of them:

◆ **Causes may have predictable and unpredictable effects.** *(When can you predict the effects of a certain cause? When can you predict that some effect will happen, but you're not sure what it will be? What are some causes that may have both predictable and unpredictable effects?)*

◆ **Causes can trigger simple effects or chains of related effects.** *(What are some examples of causes that have both* *short-term and long-term consequences or effects? What does the "domino effect" mean?)*

♦ **An effect can be the result of multiple causes with different degrees of influence.** *(What are some examples of effects that require several different causes or conditions to be met before they can happen? In your examples, are all of the causes equally important to the effect, or are some more influential than others?)*

♦ **A relationship between events that seems to be cause-effect may actually be correlational or coincidental.** *(What are some examples of events or characteristics that exist at the same time or one right after the other but are not causally related?)*

♦ **Causes have short-term and long-term effects.** *(What are some examples of short-term effects of some of your example causes? What are some examples of long-term effects?)*

♦ **Hindsight and new discoveries can help us to understand past cause and effect relationships.** *(What does hindsight mean? What are some examples of effects that you can see but can't always determine the cause right away? What are some effects whose causes are understood by scientists today but might not have been understood in the past?)*

9. Distribute copies of the **Cause and Effect Model** (Handout 2A). Have students return to their groups and use their lists of examples and non-examples, as well as what they have learned from discussion, to fill in examples that illustrate each of the generalizations.

Journal

Choose one of the generalizations about cause and effect that you think is particularly true. Write a paragraph explaining why you think it is true. Give at least three reasons or examples to show that the generalization is true.

Homework

Share the generalizations about cause and effect with someone at home. Ask them to give some examples and non-examples of cause and effect.

Extension

Explore the background of some superstitions. Where did the ideas come from? What actual cause-effect relationships might have influenced the development of the superstitions?

Notes to Teacher

1. Possible responses for the **Cause and Effect Model** are given on the **Sample Cause and Effect Model** (Teacher Resource 2). Please note, however, that the responses given are meant only as guidelines, not limits or specific responses that students must provide. Several historical examples are provided for teacher reference; students may not be familiar with the historical events indicated.

2. This lesson may take more than one class period to complete. Lessons throughout the unit will refer to the list of generalizations included in this lesson. These generalizations should be posted in the classroom, and students should keep their Cause and Effect Models in their unit folders for reference throughout the unit. Any accurate generalizations developed by students beyond the six listed should be aligned to this set and may also be posted and used for reference.

Assessment

- ◆ Participation in group discussion
- ◆ Demonstration of understanding of generalizations through model and journal responses

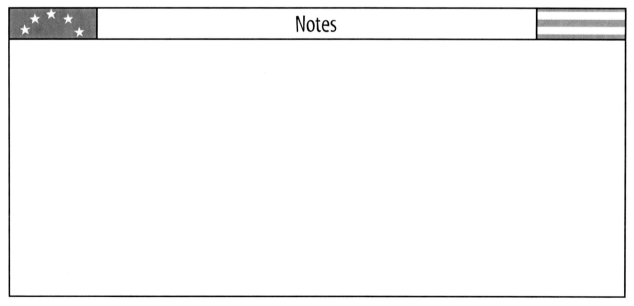

Notes

Cause and Effect Model

Give 2 to 3 examples for each generalization that show how the generalization is true.

Causes may have predictable and unpredictable effects.	Causes can trigger simple effects or chains of related effects.
An effect can be the result of multiple causes with different degrees of influence.	A relationship between events that seems to be cause-effect may actually be correlational or coincidental.
Causes have short-term and long-term effects.	Hindsight and new discoveries can help us to understand past cause and effect relationships.

Sample
Cause and Effect Model

Give 2 to 3 examples for each generalization that show how the generalization is true.

Causes may have predictable and unpredictable effects.	Causes can trigger simple effects or chains of related effects.
◆ You know the rain and wind of a hurricane will cause some property damage, but you're not sure what the specific damage will be. ◆ If you say something mean to someone, you will probably hurt their feelings, but you don't know what they might do about it. ◆ (hist) Luther's 95 Theses.	◆ When you do your science fair project, you will get credit for doing it, and you might win a prize. But you might also get more interested in a particular area of science, which may cause you to read more about that area, which may cause you to decide to take some other science courses and eventually become a scientist. ◆ (hist) beginnings of World War I
An effect can be the result of multiple causes with different degrees of influence.	**A relationship between events that seems to be cause-effect may actually be correlational or coincidental.**
◆ Flowers blooming in the spring are the effect of many causes, including planting certain seeds, having enough sun and rain, and not being choked by weeds. The planting of the seeds, though, is the most influential cause—without that, none of the others would matter. ◆ (hist) breakout of the Civil War	◆ Wearing your lucky socks on the day you got an A on a test is probably a coincidence, not a causal relationship! ◆ If someone is very interested in sports and also does very well in sports, you can't say that one of these necessarily caused the other, although they are related.
Causes have short-term and long-term effects.	**Hindsight and new discoveries can help us to understand past cause and effect relationships.**
◆ Smoking can make your breath and your clothes smell bad in the short term. In the long term, it can cause some serious health problems. ◆ (hist) Settlement at Jamestown	◆ You might notice that you have been feeling really tired lately, and you think it's because you've just been working hard and haven't gotten much sleep; but then you start sniffling and realize you were coming down with a cold. ◆ (hist) Flies thought to grow on meat until Pasteur's experiments

Lesson 3

The Stamp Act

Curriculum Alignment

Goal 1	Goal 2	Goal 3	Goal 4	Goal 5
	X		X	X

Instructional Purpose

- ◆ To identify purposes for taxation
- ◆ To analyze the reasoning behind the passage of the Stamp Act
- ◆ To analyze a primary source document
- ◆ To identify and analyze multiple points of view on an issue

Materials/Resources

1. The Stamp Act (Handout 3A)
2. Analyzing Primary Sources (Handout 3B)
3. Sentence strips

Vocabulary

debt—something that is owed, such as money, goods, or services, or the condition of owing

duty—a tax charged by a government, usually related to tax on imports

Parliament—the legislature of the United Kingdom, including the House of Lords and House of Commons, which maintained lawmaking power over British colonies

primary source—a document or other product created by someone who was present at the event or time being written about

secondary source—a document or product created by a person who was not present at the event or time being written about but is using other people's accounts and other records of an event to write about it

Stamp Act—1765 law passed in Parliament to gain funds through taxes levied on paper products in the colonies

tax—a contribution to support a government required of those persons and groups under that government's domain

📖 Activities

1. Have students begin the lesson by writing their thoughts on the following set of questions in their journals:

    ◆ *What is a tax?*

    ◆ *Who has to pay taxes?*

    ◆ *Who decides what the taxes should be?*

    ◆ *Do you think taxes are fair?*

    Tell students that they will be discussing these questions further and returning to their journal writing later in the lesson.

2. Ask students to define the term *debt*. Explain to students that when someone owes money for a good or service purchased but not fully paid for, that person has a *debt* to repay. Ask students if it is only individual people that can have debts, and explain that various larger groups and organizations, including governments, can also have debts. Ask students to think about what a government might owe money for—*what do governments have to buy and pay for?*

3. Ask students to think about the following question: *Where do governments get the money to pay their debts?* Explain that a lot of the money governments get to pay their debts comes from taxes they charge the citizens of the countries they govern.

    ◆ *Do you feel that governments should have a right to place taxes on the people? Why or why not?*

    Invite students to share their ideas. Discuss with students the kinds of organizations that today are funded by the government (including schools) and help students to understand why tax is an important aspect of government. Then ask students why a government might need to pay for the materials and personnel to fight a war, and have them brainstorm a list of the types of things that a government would need to fight a war. Explain that all these things have to be paid for—guns, ammunition, food and clothing for soldiers, paychecks for soldiers, materials and pay for other government officials, warships, materials for building forts and camps, etc. Have students return to their journal responses to the questions about what taxes are and the fairness of them, and invite them to make any revisions or additions to their responses.

4. After this introductory discussion, tell students that at the conclusion of the French and Indian War (the Seven Years' War in Europe), the English were at peace for the first time in over fifty years. However, the English government had a lot of debts to pay because of all the wars they had been involved in for the previous fifty years. In order to help pay those debts, the British Parliament, the elected law-making group of Great Britain, established a number of new taxes that the people in Great Britain and in British colonies, including the colonies in North America, would have to pay.

5. Distribute copies of **The Stamp Act** (Handout 3A) to students. Explain that this document shows some excerpts from a law that the British prime minister, George Grenville, introduced in Parliament to help raise funds for the British government. Help students to read the introductory section and the specific items from the act given on the handout.

6. Introduce **Analyzing Primary Sources** (Handout 3B). Explain that this form will help students throughout the unit as they read documents from the time period and try to understand what the documents mean and why they were important. Tell students that they will begin with this part of the form, and later in the unit they will use some additional questions for other aspects of primary source analysis. Work with students to answer the questions on the handout, following the guidelines below.

Establishing a Context and Intent for the Source

Explain to students that one of the most important parts of analyzing a primary source is to understand the context of the source—who wrote it, when, and what else was going on at the time that might have influenced the writing of the source. Ask students why they think this is an important part of the analysis. Explain that sometimes they will need to use other resources beyond the source itself to achieve this understanding of context, but that for this first experience you will provide them with the necessary background.

Author: (Explain to students that the prime minister of Great Britain was and is an important political figure who made many decisions about the government. Prime Minister George Grenville introduced the Stamp Act to Parliament in 1765, and then the members of Parliament worked on it until they had it prepared as a law.)

When was it written? (Have students note the date the Stamp Act was enacted, March 22, 1765. Explain that it was to go into effect fully for the colonies on November 1, 1765.)

Briefly describe the culture of the time and list related events of the time. (Review the recent events of the French and Indian War and discuss the fact that Britain had been at war with France and/or Spain for many years. Also review that the colonies in America were under the control of the British government.)

Purpose—Why was the document created? (Review the earlier part of the lesson in which you discussed the need for taxation to pay for the government's war debts. Also help students to understand that Parliament needed to have a written proposal of a law to discuss and vote on in order to pass it and require the tax to be paid by the people.)

Audience—Who was the document created for? (Again, explain that the way the government was organized in Great Britain, laws had to be written down so that first Parliament and then the people affected could read the law and understand it.)

Understanding the Source

Explain to students that for this part of the model, they will need to read the document carefully and come up with appropriate responses. Suggest that they may wish to underline, highlight, or make notes on their copies of the document as they come across important words and sentences.

What problems/issues/events does the document talk about? (Have students identify words and phrases in the document that indicate its purpose as well as how it is to be carried out.)

What are the main ideas? (Collecting taxes from a variety of everyday activities; make sure students understand the type of stamp the document refers to.)

What assumptions/values/feelings does the author seem to have? (What does the document show was Parliament's view on the American responsibility for helping with the war debt?)

What outcomes does the author expect? From whom? (What does Parliament expect the colonists to do?)

7. Tell students that beyond the parts of the act they read in order to respond to the primary source analysis activity, the act includes more than fifty additional statements addressing items for which the colonists would be required to pay for

stamps. Explain to students that beyond just discussing what a document actually says, in many cases historians must also seek the consequences of the document. *How did people react to it? What happened next?* Ask students to think about why these questions might be important to ask about the Stamp Act. Tell them that in the next lesson, they will be learning about what happened next with the Stamp Act of 1765.

8. Distribute some sentence strips to students and have them begin developing a unit timeline. Have students mark off each year from 1763 to 1783 on sentence strips, leaving room to write information related to each year. Have students note the end of the French and Indian War and the Stamp Act on their timelines.

Journal

If you were an American colonist in 1765, what do you think your reaction to the Stamp Act would have been? Why? If you were a British person living in London in 1765, what do you think your reaction to the Stamp Act would have been? Why?

Homework

Have you ever had an experience in which it was really important to understand two sides of a story? Or have you ever read a book or seen a movie in which you got a better understanding of what was going on when you heard both sides? Write a few paragraphs to summarize your experience or a story in which it was really important to understand both sides.

Notes to Teacher

1. The model for analyzing primary sources used in this lesson is a portion of a larger model to be incorporated throughout the unit. The model is explained in more detail in the implementation section.

2. The Stamp Act is given here in its original form, without simplification of language. Students are likely to need some assistance in understanding the language of the document; however, as the intent is to focus on primary source analysis, they should have the experience of trying to read the original. To provide some assistance, several key sections of the first part of the document are given in **bold** print on the handout.

3. Students should maintain their timelines in their notebooks throughout the course of the unit. A class timeline should also be posted in the room for reference. A sample timeline listing major items to be included appears in Section III of the unit; the sample is not an exhaustive list, however, and students' final timelines may include many other items not listed on the sample.

Assessment

♦ Responses to discussion
♦ Journal response

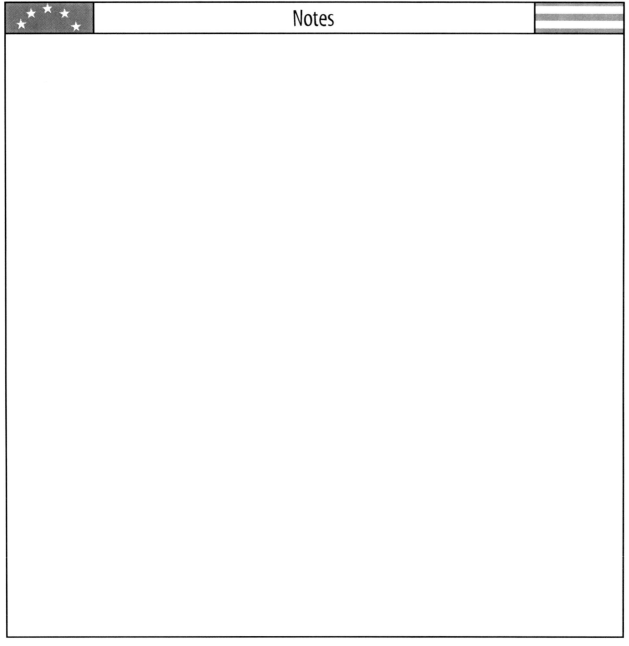

Notes

The Stamp Act
(Excerpt)

March 22, 1765

AN ACT for **granting and applying certain stamp duties, and other duties, in the British colonies and plantations in America, towards further defraying the expences of defending, protecting, and securing the same;** and for amending such parts of the several acts of parliament relating to the trade and revenues of the said colonies and plantations, as direct the manner of determining and recovering the penalties and forfeitures therein mentioned.

WHEREAS, by an act made in the last session of Parliament several duties were granted, continued, and appropriated toward defraying the expenses of defending, protecting, and securing the British colonies and plantations in America; and whereas **it is just and necessary that provision be made for raising a further revenue within your majesty's dominions in America toward defraying the said expenses;** we, your majesty's most dutiful and loyal subjects, the Commons of Great Britain, in Parliament assembled, have therefore resolved to give and grant unto your majesty the several rates and duties hereinafter mentioned; and do humbly beseech your majesty that it may be enacted, and be it enacted by the king's most excellent majesty, by and with the advice and consent of the lords spiritual and temporal, and commons, in this present Parliament assembled, and by the authority of the same, that **from and after the first day of November, one thousand seven hundred and sixty five, there shall be raised, levied, collected, and paid unto his majesty, his heirs, and successors, throughout the colonies and plantations in America,** which now are, or hereafter may be, under the dominion of his majesty, his heirs and successors:

1. For every skin or piece of vellum or parchment, or sheet or piece of paper, on which shall be engrossed, written, or printed, any declaration, plea, replication, rejoinder, demurrer or other pleading, or any copy thereof; in any court of law within the British colonies and plantations in America, a stamp duty of three pence. . . .

42. And for and upon every pack of playing cards, and all dice, which shall be sold or used within the said colonies and plantations, the several stamp duties following (that is to say):

43. For every pack of such cards, one shilling.

44. And for every pair of such dice, ten shillings.

45. And for and every paper called a pamphlet, and upon every newspaper, containing public news or occurrences, which shall be printed, dispersed, and made public, within any of the said colonies and plantations, and for and upon such advertisements as are hereinafter mentioned, the respective duties following (that is to say):

46. For every such pamphlet and paper contained in a half sheet, or any lesser piece of paper, which shall be so printed, a stamp duty of one half penny for every printed copy thereof.

47. For every such pamphlet and paper (being larger than half a sheet, and not exceeding one whole sheet), which shall be printed, a stamp duty of one penny for every printed copy thereof. . . .

Name_____ Date _____

Analyzing Primary Sources

Document Title:_____

Establishing a Context and Intent for the Source

> Author:
>
> Time (When was it written)?
>
> Briefly describe the culture of the time and list related events of the time.
>
> Purpose (Why was the document created?)
>
> Audience (Who was the document created for?)

Understanding the Source

> What problems/issues/events does the source address?
>
> What are the main points/ideas/arguments?
>
> What assumptions/values/feelings does the author reflect?
>
> What actions/outcomes does the author expect? From whom?

The Stamp Act, Part 2: The American Reaction

Curriculum Alignment

Goal 1	Goal 2	Goal 3	Goal 4	Goal 5
X	X	X	X	X

Instructional Purpose

- ◆ To identify and explore multiple points of view on an issue
- ◆ To analyze a primary source document
- ◆ To explain the arguments of the American colonists regarding taxation without representation

Materials/Resources

1. Scenario (Handout 4A)
2. Stamp Act Resolutions (Handout 4B)
3. Analyzing Primary Sources (Handout 4C)
4. Reasoning about a Situation or Event (Handout 4D)

Vocabulary

assumption—something that is taken for granted or accepted as true without proof

implication—a suggestion of likely or logical consequence; a logical relationship between two linked propositions or statements

representation—the condition of serving as an official delegate or spokesperson of the interests of a group, especially to a legislative body

riot—a violent disturbance of the public peace by a group of people

tyranny—absolute power in a government; actions demonstrating absolute power, especially unjust or cruel actions

Activities

1. Ask students to share responses from their journal activity in the previous lesson addressing how they think they might have reacted to the Stamp Act if they had been American colonists living in 1765. Ask them how they think their homework assignment, addressing multiple points of view on an issue, relates to the events of 1765.

2. Tell students that reactions to the Stamp Act in the American colonies were very strong and in some cases violent. Many colonists protested the Stamp Act in writing and in speeches, and in some colonies, riots broke out, with officials of the British government threatened and their houses ransacked. And yet, only a decade earlier, three of the colonial assemblies or local governments had imposed stamp taxes to help pay for the French and Indian War, and stamp taxes had been common in England for a long time. *Why were the colonists so angry about the tax?*

3. Post the following quote, based on the writings and commentary of James Otis, Patrick Henry, and others, on the board or overhead: "Taxation without Representation is Tyranny." Ask students if they can define first the terms of the statement, then the meaning of the statement itself. Provide definitions of the terms as needed.

4. Explain to students that in the form of government practiced by Great Britain, the Parliament, which was responsible for making laws, was partially elected by the citizens of Great Britain. This meant that the members of Parliament had an obligation to represent the needs and perspectives of the people who had elected them, or else the people would elect someone else who was a better representative. Give students the example of student government, if they are familiar with such a structure in the school, in which one or two students from a class participate in a student government structure that does some decision-making for the whole school, and the representatives are expected to think about what is best for the students in their class and in the whole school in the decisions they make.

5. Distribute copies of the **Scenario** (Handout 4A) and ask students to discuss the questions in small groups. Then debrief as a class, asking students how they would feel differently about decisions made by a student government with a representative from their class versus a student government with-

out a representative. Explain that this lack of representation was the colonists' main argument against the Stamp Act; they did not have a representative with an influential vote in Parliament, so they felt it was unfair for this tax to be imposed on them. They also had some specific ideas about the kinds of taxes they felt Parliament should be able to impose and the kinds they felt Parliament should not.

6. Tell students that at the suggestion of some colonial leaders in Massachusetts, nine of the colonies sent representatives to a Stamp Act Congress, which discussed the problem and developed a set of resolutions about the Stamp Act that they sent to Parliament to express their opinions. Have students read the excerpts from the **Stamp Act Resolutions** (Handout 4B) and work in groups to complete **Analyzing Primary Sources** (Handout 4C).

7. Explain to students that in the last two lessons, they have read documents and discussed the background on both sides of the Stamp Act issue. Explain that when we think about an issue or problem, it is important to think about different points of view about that issue or problem, because it helps us to understand the overall problem and the possible consequences of different decisions better. Introduce **Reasoning about a Situation or Event** (Handout 4D). Tell students that this chart will help them organize their thoughts about the different stakeholders, or people who care, about a certain issue or event and why those stakeholders have the opinions they do on the event. Work with students to complete the chart about the Stamp Act issue, using the questions that follow as a guide. (Additional columns may be added to the chart as needed.)

    ◆ *What is the situation? (What is the problem we are thinking about? Why are we thinking about it? When and where did the problem arise?)*

    ◆ *Who are the stakeholders? (Who were the groups of people that cared about the Stamp Act issue? Parliament, British people, American colonists, merchants, etc.)*

    ◆ *What is the point of view for each stakeholder? (Point of view is the opinion or way someone thinks about an issue or problem. What did the different stakeholders think about the problem of the Stamp Act? What did they stand to gain or lose from the situation? Why did they care about the problem?)*

- *What are the assumptions of each group? (Assumptions are the fundamental understandings that underlie our point of view about an issue. Our assumptions are based on our experiences and our cultural ways of thinking. In the case of the Stamp Act, what understandings about government underlie the different points of view? What understandings about colonialism underlie the different points of view? How were the assumptions about British citizenship different among the members of Parliament and the colonists?)*

- *What are the implications of these views? (Implications are the possible consequences or outcomes of actions related to different points of view. Ask students to think about what might have been the implications of the different points of view and to write on their charts what the implications were.)*

8. Tell students that as they work through the unit, they will have more opportunities to practice this way of thinking about a problem. Remind students to mark the Stamp Act Resolutions on their timelines.

Journal

Do you think the *effects* of the passage of the Stamp Act were predictable or unpredictable for Parliament? Do you think the members of Parliament expected such a strong reaction from the colonists? Why or why not?

Homework

Imagine that you are either a member of Parliament or an American colonist in the summer of 1765. Think about what your point of view on the Stamp Act issue would have been, and write a sentence explaining your point of view and three or more sentences explaining your reasons.

Notes to Teacher

1. The **Reasoning about a Situation or Event** activity introduced in this lesson is an application of the Reasoning Model that will be used throughout the unit. The purpose of this particular activity is to recognize the influence of multiple perspectives on situations in history, and to help students recognize how our assumptions affect our point of view on issues and our decisions.

2. The **Scenario** provided in Handout 4A is an extreme simplification of the taxation without representation issue, but it is intended to help students contextualize the ideas.

3. The handout of the **Stamp Act Resolutions** has been excerpted to focus primarily on the objections to the Stamp Act itself and briefly on other Parliamentary restrictions on commerce; the resolutions also included reference to other acts, but they are excluded here to try to simplify the analysis somewhat for students.

4. This lesson is likely to take more than one class period to complete; a good break point is after students read the Stamp Act Resolutions, but before they work through the **Reasoning about a Situation or Event** chart.

Assessment

- ◆ Responses in discussion
- ◆ Primary Source Analysis
- ◆ Situation chart

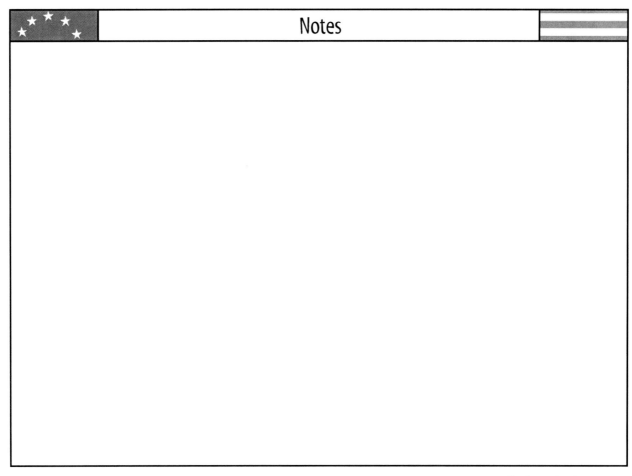

Notes

Scenario

The principal of your school has decided to make some changes in how student government works. He wants to get a better understanding of how the students feel about issues in the school and give students a chance to help make some decisions about how the school uses resources and the types of activities the school plans. He is going to form a special student advisory committee to consult with him about some of these decisions.

The principal wants to be able to call his student advisory committee in at a moment's notice to discuss issues and decisions. Your school's intercom is out of order and you have been waiting for a few months for someone to come to fix it. It is winter time, and the principal hates to go outside in the cold. So he has decided that for now, he will select his student advisory committee only from classrooms close to his office, so that he can reach the students quickly and easily to call them for meetings.

Your class is located in a portable unit. You know that no one in your class will be selected for the student advisory committee because no one wants to walk all the way to the portables to call you for meetings.

How do you feel about this situation?

Do you think your class's interests will be fairly represented by other students on the advisory committee? Why or why not?

What would you recommend to the principal as another way of handling this situation?

Stamp Act Resolutions
(Excerpts)

October 19, 1765

The members of this Congress, sincerely devoted, with the warmest sentiments of affection and duty to His Majesty's Person and Government . . . ; having considered as maturely as time will permit the circumstances of the said colonies, esteem it our indispensable duty to make the following declarations of our humble opinion, respecting the most essential rights and liberties of the colonists, and of the grievances under which they labour, by reason of several late Acts of Parliament.

I. That His Majesty's subjects in these colonies, owe the same allegiance to the Crown of Great-Britain, that is owing from his subjects born within the realm, and all due subordination to that august body the Parliament of Great Britain.

II. That His Majesty's liege subjects in these colonies, are entitled to all the inherent rights and liberties of his natural born subjects within the kingdom of Great-Britain.

III. That it is inseparably essential to the freedom of a people, and the undoubted right of Englishmen, that no taxes be imposed on them, but with their own consent, given personally, or by their representatives.

IV. That the people of these colonies are not, and from their local circumstances cannot be, represented in the House of Commons in Great-Britain. . . .

VIII. That the late Act of Parliament, entitled, An Act for granting and applying certain Stamp Duties, and other Duties, in the British colonies and plantations in America, etc., by imposing taxes on the inhabitants of these colonies . . . ha[s] a manifest tendency to subvert the rights and liberties of the colonists.

IX. That the duties imposed by several late Acts of Parliament, from the peculiar circumstances of these colonies, will be extremely burthensome and grievous; and from the scarcity of specie, the payment of them absolutely impracticable. . . .

XII. That the increase, prosperity, and happiness of these colonies, depend on the full and free enjoyment of their rights and liberties, and an intercourse with Great-Britain mutually affectionate and advantageous.

XIII. That it is the right of the British subjects in these colonies, to petition the King, Or either House of Parliament.

Lastly, That it is the indispensable duty of these colonies, to the best of sovereigns, to the mother country, and to themselves, to endeavour by a loyal and dutiful address to his Majesty, and humble applications to both Houses of Parliament, to procure the repeal of the Act for granting and applying certain stamp duties . . . and of the other late Acts for the restriction of American commerce.

Name_____ Date _____ H a n d o u t

Analyzing Primary Sources

Document Title:_____

Establishing a Context and Intent for the Source

Author:

Time (When was it written)?

Briefly describe the culture of the time and list related events of the time.

Purpose (Why was the document created?)

Audience (Who was the document created for?)

Understanding the Source

What problems/issues/events does the source address?

What are the main points/ideas/arguments?

What assumptions/values/feelings does the author reflect?

What actions/outcomes does the author expect? From whom?

Reasoning About a Situation or Event

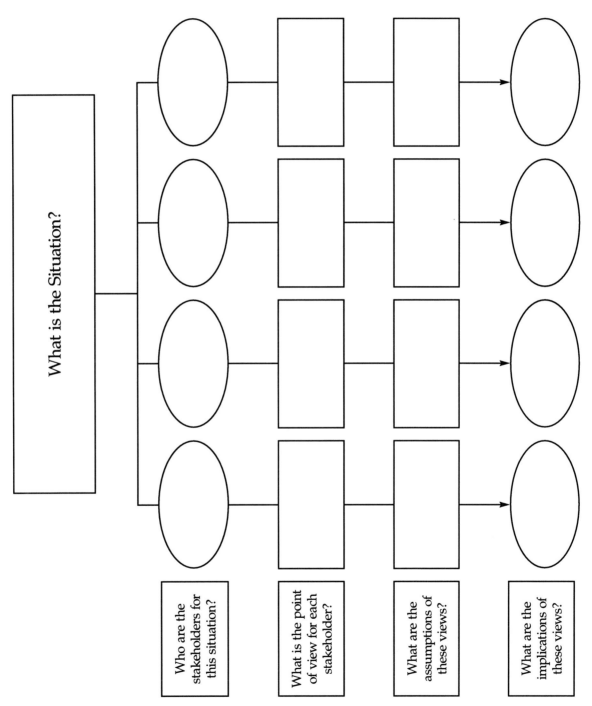

What is the Situation?

Who are the stakeholders for this situation?

What is the point of view for each stakeholder?

What are the assumptions of these views?

What are the implications of these views?

Lesson 5

Persuasive Writing

Curriculum Alignment

Goal 1	Goal 2	Goal 3	Goal 4	Goal 5
	X			X

Instructional Purpose

- ◆ To use historical fiction to explore life in the Revolutionary period
- ◆ To introduce a model for persuasive writing
- ◆ To explore points of view on the Stamp Act issue

Materials/Resources

1. Historical Fiction Assignment (Handout 5A)
2. Books for historical fiction assignment
3. Hamburger Model for Persuasive Writing (Handout 5B)
4. Vacations at the Beach (Handout 5C)
5. No Vacations at the Beach (Handout 5D)
6. Crayons
7. Scissors

Vocabulary

historical fiction—a literary work that recreates a period or event in history, often using both fictional and actual characters

persuasive writing—a form of writing designed to convince the reader of the author's point of view on an issue

Activities

1. Explain to students that as they work through this unit, they will have several different kinds of opportunities to think about the events surrounding the American Revolution, what life was like during the period, and the different perspectives people had about what was happening around them. One of the ways they will develop an understanding of the period will be to read historical fiction taking place during the time and to discuss how it relates to the historical information they learn through their lessons and discussion of documents. Distribute copies of the **Historical Fiction Assignment** (Handout 5A) and go over with students. Assign books and a date for completion of the stages of the assignment. (Students should have their books at least partially complete by Lesson 14 and should have completed their reading before Lesson 17.)

2. Remind students of their homework from the previous lesson in which they were asked to give reasons supporting a point of view about the Stamp Act Crisis. Explain that in this lesson, they will be learning a way of organizing their writing when they want to share an opinion about something and give reasons for their opinion. Tell students that this type of writing, in which we are trying to convince someone about our point of view, is called *persuasive writing*.

3. Introduce the **Hamburger Model for Persuasive Writing** (Handout 5B). Tell students that this is a good way to think about their writing, because it helps to remind them of the pieces they need. Explain that in the Hamburger Model, the top bun of the hamburger is the main idea sentence, in which they will share their point of view. The meat of the hamburger is the reasons for their opinion. The "fixings" of the hamburger, or the lettuce, tomato, pickles, cheese, and condiments, are the parts that make the hamburger more interesting; in writing, they are the parts that elaborate on, or give more details and examples about, the reasons. The bottom bun is a conclusion statement that wraps up the piece of writing and restates the opinion. This model can be used to describe a persuasive paragraph or a longer persuasive essay.

4. Give students the sample paragraph on **Vacations at the Beach** (Handout 5C). Ask them to read the paragraph, then help them to identify the pieces of the Hamburger Model in the paragraph. Have them circle the top bun or introduction/opinion statement with a light brown crayon, the reasons or "meat" sentences with a darker brown or black crayon; the

elaboration sentences with red, green, yellow, or orange crayons; and the bottom bun or concluding statement with the light brown crayon.

5. Give students the jumbled paragraph on **No Vacations at the Beach** (Handout 5D) and a copy of the Hamburger Model. Ask them to cut the jumbled paragraph into sentence strips, then rearrange the sentences in the correct order and glue them to the blank Hamburger Model.

6. Tell students that they can use the point of view and reasons they wrote about the Stamp Act crisis to write Hamburger Paragraphs. Invite students to use their copy of the model or a copy they draw on their paper as a graphic organizer to plan their paragraphs. Remind them that in addition to a strong point of view statement, three good reasons, and a conclusion, they should provide examples or details to elaborate on their reasons.

7. Tell students that they can use the sentences they filled into the model as a "sloppy copy" or rough draft of their writing, from which they can make a clean final copy. Remind students of the basics of paragraph writing, such as that they should indent the first sentence and use correct capitalization and punctuation at the beginnings and ends of their sentences. Have students complete their paragraphs and invite them to share their work.

Homework

Share the Hamburger Model with someone at home. Write a paragraph to try to persuade someone at home of something you want and share the pieces of the paragraph.

Notes to Teacher

1. The three novels about the Revolutionary period vary in difficulty and should be assigned to students based on appropriate challenge level, as well as interest. Avi's *The Fighting Ground* is the easiest of the books, while the other two are more difficult. In keeping with their subject, all three books contain some disturbing events; be sure to preview the books before assigning them to students. You may wish to schedule time for students to meet in "literature circles" based on the book they are reading during the unit, so that they can discuss the questions and their responses as they go along.

2. This lesson may be used as a social studies lesson or as a language arts lesson. Based on time available, you may also wish to add a peer review and revision stage to the lesson between the Hamburger Model and the final copy. Also, you may want to set up a writing center in the classroom related to the unit, with suggested prompts for students to engage in persuasive writing about key issues related to what they are studying.

3. You may wish to have students write their first Hamburger Paragraph about an issue they are thinking about in school instead of starting off with the Stamp Act issue, or you may wish to have them write their Stamp Act paragraphs in groups, just to provide support in getting used to the model while also grappling with the content.

4. The Hamburger Model and its more advanced adaptation, the Dagwood Model, are outlined in the implementation section at the end of the unit.

Assessment

- ◆ Rearranged jumbled paragraphs
- ◆ Completed Hamburger Model paragraphs

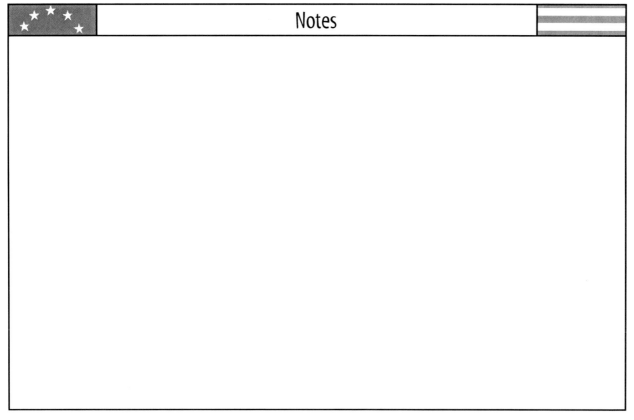

Historical Fiction Assignment

As part of your work in this unit on the American Revolution, you will be reading a novel that takes place during the Revolutionary period. You will select from the following list of novels and complete the assignments given below by _____ (date).

>   *The Fighting Ground* by Avi
>   *My Brother Sam is Dead* by J. Collier and C. Collier
>   *Sarah Bishop* by Scott O'Dell

As you read the novel, keep a reading journal. About every 40 to 50 pages, write responses to the following questions:

♦   What important events of the Revolution have your characters experienced?

♦   How did the events involve or affect them?

♦   How did their experiences relate to what you learned about those events?

♦   What issues or problems did your characters have to face? What point of view did the main character take on these issues?

♦   What details about daily life did you learn?

When you finish the novel, write responses to the following questions:

- ◆ Were your main characters Patriots or Tories? What assumptions and ideas influenced their ways of thinking about this decision? How did their views change throughout the novel?

- ◆ Predict what will happen to your main characters after the Revolution.

- ◆ How did the novel affect your understanding of the Revolutionary period?

When you have finished your novel, you will give a presentation to the class reviewing the novel and using the Hamburger Model to share your point of view on whether you would or would not recommend the book to others.

Name _____ Date _____

Hamburger Model for Persuasive Writing

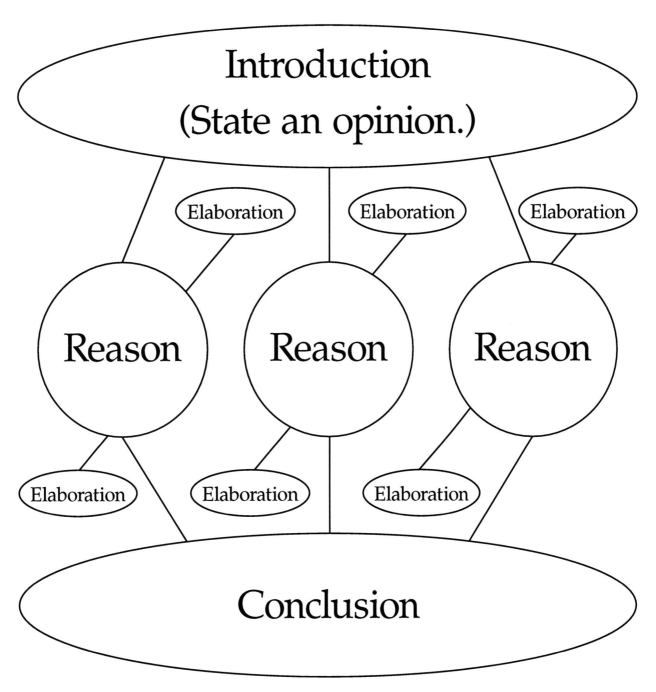

Vacations at the Beach

Vacations at the beach are my favorite kinds of vacations. You can play in the water and dive under the waves. Since the waves are always moving, swimming in the ocean is more interesting and exciting than swimming in a pool. I also think it is really fun to build sand castles on the beach. You can build them as big as you like, and then you can imagine all kinds of adventures to happen in them! Sometimes, you can find many interesting sea shells and other things from the ocean on the sand. These can make a really good collection or great souvenirs to bring home as gifts to friends. Those are the reasons why vacations at the beach are the best!

No Vacations at the Beach

Sometimes that can make you feel a little sick.

Finally, when you build a great sand castle, the water always comes and knocks it down.

Also, you get a sunburn when you spend the day at the beach.

I do not like vacations at the beach.

Those are the reasons why I think vacations at the beach are no fun.

After you've spent all day working on something, it's pretty depressing to have it destroyed so quickly.

First, when you swim at the beach, you always get salt water in your mouth.

Then your skin hurts for days and sometimes it peels.

Growing Discontent: Taxes and Tea

Lesson 6

Curriculum Alignment

Goal 1	Goal 2	Goal 3	Goal 4	Goal 5
X	X	X	X	X

Instructional Purpose

- ◆ To outline the chronology of events following the Stamp Act crisis and contributing to growing hostilities
- ◆ To analyze the purposes and infer outcomes of Acts of Parliament
- ◆ To analyze the influence of perspective on different accounts of an event
- ◆ To analyze primary source documents

Materials/Resources

1. Summaries of Acts of Parliament (Handout 6A)
2. Analysis of an Act (Handout 6B)
3. Resources on the pre-Revolutionary period
4. The Boston Massacre (Handout 6C)
5. Internet access OR print copy of Paul Revere's engraving of the Boston Massacre
6. The Boston Tea Party (Handout 6D)
7. Reasoning about the Tea Party (Handout 6E)

Vocabulary

huzza—a shout or loud cry, used to express joy or triumph

massacre—the killing of a large number of people, usually very cruelly and with helpless or unresisting victims

patriot—one who loves, defends, or protects his or her country and supports its authority

propaganda—the deliberate spreading of ideas, information, or rumor to support a cause or damage an opposing cause

quartering—providing housing, especially for military troops

repeal—to revoke or cancel a law or act through another official act

Activities

1. Tell students that after the crisis surrounding the Stamp Act and because of all the protest that followed the act, Parliament repealed or cancelled the Stamp Act in March, 1766. (Students can view the print of the famous satire "The Repeal, or the Funeral of Miss Ame-Stamp" at *http://www.loc.gov/exhibits/british/images/vc35.jpg*.) However, Parliament also passed a number of other taxes that affected the daily lives of the colonists.

2. Divide students into five groups. Assign each group one of the following acts of Parliament to think about: the Sugar Act of 1764, the Townshend Act of 1767, the Quartering Act of 1765, the Declaratory Act of 1767, and the Tea Act of 1773. Distribute copies of **Summaries of Acts of Parliament** (Handout 6A) and ask each group of students to read the summary of their act and then to discuss and complete **Analysis of an Act** (Handout 6B). (Have additional resources on the pre-Revolutionary period available as well, in case students need additional background on their acts to support their discussion. Some general resources are listed in the resources section at the end of the unit.)

3. Reorganize students into different groups so that each group now has one person from each of the previous groups (jigsaw). In these groups, have students discuss their analysis sheets from the previous group so that each student has an opportunity to understand all five acts.

4. Tell students that many colonists continued to have strong negative reactions to these acts of Parliament and continued to feel that the British government's taxation policies were unfair. Plus, the colonists were unhappy with the many British troops that were stationed in their towns and sometimes quartered in their homes. The city of Boston, Massachusetts, was one of the places with the most problems related to protests from colonists and conflict between colonists and British troops.

5. Ask students if they have heard of an event known as the Boston Massacre. Ask students to define the term massacre. Then have them read **The Boston Massacre** (Handout 6C). Ask students to consider the following questions:

   ◆ *Do you think this event was really a "massacre"? Why or why not?*

   ◆ *Why do you think it is referred to as a massacre?*

6. Give students an opportunity to view the Revere engraving of the Boston Massacre. Reprints of this picture appear in many textbooks on the colonial and Revolutionary period, and it may also be viewed on line at *http://www.loc.gov/exhibits/british/images/vc38.jpg*. Ask students the following questions:

   ◆ *What do you think was the artist's purpose in showing the event in this way?*

   ◆ *What does **propaganda** mean?*

   ◆ *What ideas and assumptions about the British soldiers does the print promote?*

   ◆ *What ideas and assumptions about the colonists does it promote?*

7. Tell students that the Boston Massacre was used as a rallying cry for the Patriots, or the American colonists who were protesting the acts of Parliament. Explain that tensions continued to exist between the colonists and the British, although Parliament repealed many of the taxes that had been passed under the Townshend Acts. However, one of the taxes that remained an issue over the next several years was the tax on tea.

8. Have students return to the song they read in Lesson 1. Tell students that it refers to the final act on their list from earlier in this lesson, the Tea Act, and the colonial reaction to it. Ask students if they have heard the story of the Boston Tea Party. Explain that in protest of the Tea Act, the ships of tea sent by the British East India Company had been turned away from Philadelphia and New York, but the Governor of Massachusetts insisted that the tea should be brought into Boston harbor. The colonists tried to negotiate with the governor, but were unable to get time with him to discuss it. Have students read **The Boston Tea Party** (Handout 6D) and view the painting at *http://www.loc.gov/exhibits/british/images/ vc40.jpg*. Ask students to think about whether this action on the part of the colonists was a fair or appropriate one. Distribute copies of **Reasoning about the Tea Party** (Handout 6E) and work with students to consider this issue.

9. Encourage students to add events discussed in this lesson to their unit timelines.

Journal

Think about the acts of Parliament you have been studying and the events of the Boston Massacre and Boston Tea Party. How do these events relate to the generalization that causes can trigger simple effects or chains of related effects? Write or diagram some of the causes and effects related to the events we have been studying.

Homework

Imagine that you are a colonist living in Boston in 1773. Use a Hamburger Model diagram to plan a persuasive paragraph to explain whether you think the group of protesters should or should not have dumped the British tea into the harbor. Then write a rough draft of your paragraph.

Extensions

Several contemporary accounts of the Boston Massacre are available on-line. Have students read the "anonymous account" at *http://www.ukans.edu/carrie/docs/texts/bostanon.html*, Captain Preston's account at *http://odur.let.rug.nl/~usa/D/1751-1775/boston-massacre/prest.htm*, and John Hancock's "Boston Massacre Oration," delivered on the fourth anniversary of the event, at *http://douglass.speech.nwu.edu/hanc_a49.htm*. Then have students discuss why they think these different documents portray the event in such different ways. Why do they emphasize the aspects they do?

Notes to Teacher

1. The Library of Congress has some information about the tensions between Britain and the colonies on line at *http://www.loc.gov/exhibits/british/brit-2.html*, including summary information and several prints referenced in this lesson and others.

2. This lesson is likely to take more than one class period to complete. A suggested division point is after the discussion of the Boston Massacre.

Assessment

- Participation in discussion
- Sharing of information in jigsaw activity
- Reasoning chart
- Journal response

Summaries of Acts of Parliament

1764—The **Sugar Act** required strict enforcement of duties on imports of sugar and molasses from the West Indies. It was passed to help offset the war debt brought on by the French and Indian War and to help pay for the expenses of running the colonies and newly acquired territories. Other items taxed under the Sugar Act included textiles, coffee, wines, and indigo.

1765—The **Quartering Act,** passed in March of 1765, required colonists to provide food and housing for British troops. Although the act was supposedly intended to help protect the colonists from the Indians, most of the troops were stationed in the coastal cities, such as New York and Boston, not on the frontier where interaction with the Indians was greater.

1766—On the same day it repealed the Stamp Act, the English Parliament passed the **Declaratory Act,** stating that the British government has total power to legislate any laws governing the American colonies.

1767—In June, the English Parliament passed the **Townshend Acts,** which taxed imports of such items as paper, glass, paint, lead, and tea. These taxes were intended to help offset the administration costs for the British of governing the colonies. The act also established a colonial board of customs commissioners in Boston.

1773—The **Tea Act** took effect in May. This act maintained a previous tea tax, but exempted the British East India Company from it so that the company could sell its tea more cheaply in the colonies than other merchants, including colonial merchants who had been smuggling tea from Holland to avoid the taxes. The East India Company, which was nearly bankrupt and had millions of pounds of unused tea in its warehouses, had successfully lobbied Parliament for this act. In September, Parliament authorized the company to ship half a million pounds of tea to a group of chosen tea agents.

Sources: *http://www.historyplace.com/unitedstates/revolution/rev-prel.htm;* Gordon, *American History;* Fleming, *Liberty! The American Revolution.*

Handout

6B

Analysis of an Act

	Sugar Act (1764)	Quartering Act (1765)	Declaratory Act (1766)	Townshend Acts (1767)	Tea Act (1773)
What the act stated					
Purpose of the act					
Possible implications for Britain					
Possible implications for the colonies					

The Boston Massacre

Tensions between the colonists of Boston and the British troops grew from the time the large group of soldiers arrived in 1768. Bostonians jeered at the soldiers in the streets, calling them "lobsters" and "bloody-backs" because of their red coats. British soldiers raced their horses or played military marches outside Boston churches on Sunday mornings. Tavern brawls occurred many nights between the soldiers and the colonists. Propaganda, including newspapers and posters, exaggerated any negative actions of the British troops.

On the evening of March 5, 1770, a group of angry Bostonians confronted eight British soldiers guarding the Customs House. They teased and taunted the soldiers, and some threw snow, garbage, and oyster shells at them. Some reports say that some of the colonists threatened the soldiers with sticks and dared them to fire. Finally, frightened by the crowd, the soldiers fired their guns, and five of the Bostonians were killed.

The city responded angrily to the event, especially after Paul Revere's famous engraving appeared. This engraving, titled "The Bloody Massacre Perpetrated in King Street, Boston on March 5, 1770," showed the event in a way that emphasized the gunfire but none of the mob actions that preceded it. The royal governor, Thomas Hutchinson, had the soldiers arrested, and they were tried in the fall of 1770. The soldiers were defended by local attorneys John Adams and Josiah Quincy, who were part of the colonial protest movement, but hoped to show that the leaders of the protest movement wished to work out problems legally. Six of the eight soldiers were acquitted. However, many colonists continued to talk about the "Boston Massacre" as an example of the unfair and oppressive actions of the British against the Americans.

The Boston Tea Party

(From an account written by George Hewes, a Boston cobbler and participant in the Tea Party, 1773.)

. . . On the day preceding the seventeenth, there was a meeting . . . for the purpose of consulting on what measures might be considered expedient to prevent the landing of the tea, or secure the people from the collection of the duty. At that meeting a committee was appointed to wait on Governor Hutchinson, and request him to inform them whether he would take any measures to satisfy the people. . . . When the committee returned and informed the meeting of the absence of the Governor, there was a confused murmur among the members, and the meeting was immediately dissolved, many of them crying out, "Let every man do his duty, and be true to his country"; and there was a general huzza for Griffin's wharf.

It was now evening, and I immediately dressed myself in the costume of an Indian, equipped with a small hatchet, which I and my associates denominated the tomahawk, with which, and a club, after having painted my face and hands with coal dust in the shop of a blacksmith, I repaired to Griffin's wharf, where the ships lay that contained the tea. When I first appeared in the street after being thus disguised, I fell in with many who were dressed, equipped, and painted as I was, and who fell in with me and marched in order to the place of our destination.

When we arrived at the wharf, there were three of our number who assumed an authority to direct our operations, to which we readily submitted. They divided us into three parties, for the purpose of boarding the three ships. . . . We then were ordered by our commander to open the hatches and take out all the chests of tea and throw them overboard, and we immediately proceeded to execute his orders, first cutting and splitting the chests with our tomahawks, so as thoroughly to expose them to the effects of the water. In about three hours from the time we went on board, we had thus broken and thrown overboard every tea chest to be found in the ship, while those in the other ships were disposing of the tea in the same way, at the same time. We were surrounded by British armed ships, but no attempt was made to resist us.

We then quietly retired to our several places of residence, without having any conversation with each other, or taking any measures to discover who were our associates. . . . There appeared to be an understanding that each individual should volunteer his services, keep his own secret, and risk the consequence for himself. No disorder took place during that transaction, and it was observed at that time that the stillest night ensued that Boston had enjoyed for many months. . . .

The next morning, after we had cleared the ships of the tea, it was discovered that very considerable quantities of it were floating upon the surface of the water; and to prevent the possibility of any of its being saved for use, a number of small boats were manned by sailors and citizens, who rowed them into those parts of the harbor wherever the tea was visible, and by beating it with oars and paddles so thoroughly drenched it as to render its entire destruction inevitable.

Source: Monk, *Ordinary Americans,* pp. 26–28.

Reasoning about the Tea Party

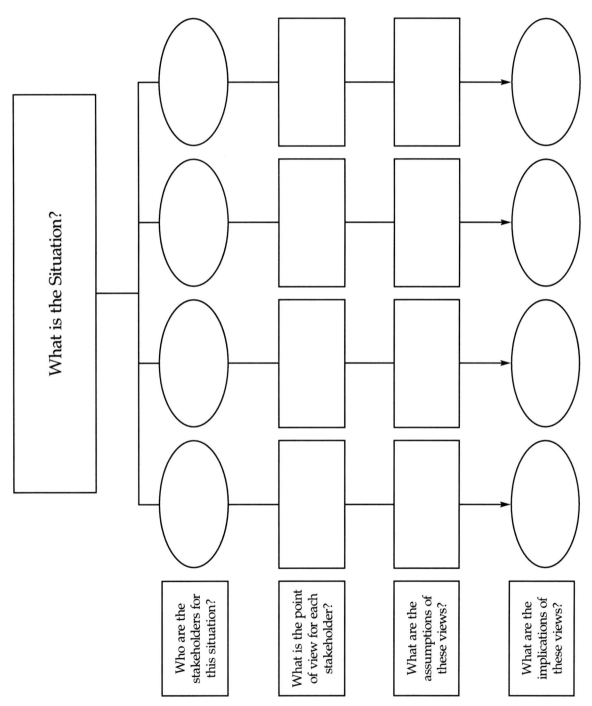

What is the Situation?

Who are the stakeholders for this situation?

What is the point of view for each stakeholder?

What are the assumptions of these views?

What are the implications of these views?

The Revolution Begins: Lexington and Concord

Curriculum Alignment

Goal 1	Goal 2	Goal 3	Goal 4	Goal 5
X	X		X	X

 ## Instructional Purpose

- ◆ To discuss changing colonial perspectives of America and its relationship to Britain
- ◆ To discuss and understand events leading to and during the battles of Lexington and Concord
- ◆ To analyze a primary source account of the events at Lexington
- ◆ To use maps to understand events and situations

Materials/Resources

1. Map of the 13 Colonies (Handout 7A)
2. Quotes from the First Continental Congress (Handout 7B)
3. Map of Boston, Lexington, and Concord (Handout 7C)
4. Lexington (Handout 7D)
5. Analyzing Primary Sources (Handout 7E)
6. The Shot Heard 'Round the World (Handout 7F)

Vocabulary

constitution—the system of laws or principles that prescribes the nature, functions, and limits of a government

intolerable—unbearable, impossible to endure or accept

militia—an army of ordinary citizens, not professional soldiers; organized armed forces called on only in emergency

Activities

1. Have students work in pairs to read and comment on one another's rough drafts from the homework in the previous lesson. Explain to students that they should consider the comments from their peers in preparing a revised draft of the paragraph, and that their revision should also take the form of a letter directed to a Boston newspaper in 1773 (still maintaining the Hamburger Model structure). Allow students time as available to get started but ask them to complete their letters for homework.

2. Distribute copies of **Map of the 13 Colonies** (Handout 7A) to students and have them look it over. Have students compare the map to a current map of the United States and locate where the original 13 colonies were located. Have them also identify on their colonial map the major cities of the colonies: Boston, New York, Philadelphia, and Charleston. Explain that each of these cities was an important location for many reasons, including their ports, which supported trade, and their large populations.

3. Have students recall study they have done of the colonial period and the three major regions of the colonies: New England, the middle colonies, and the southern colonies. Explain that each individual colony had its own colonial government, all under Great Britain, and that the colonies had different degrees of reaction to the acts of Parliament we have been discussing. Based on the events previously discussed, ask students to think about where most of the publicized negative reaction to the acts of Parliament was occurring. Explain that New England and particularly Massachusetts were the center of the action. Tell students that following the Boston Tea Party, Parliament passed a set of four acts that increased British power in Massachusetts and closed the port of Boston. Ask students the following questions:

   ◆ *What are the implications of these acts for the people of Massachusetts?*

   ◆ *How do you think the other colonies might have reacted?*

   ◆ *These acts of Parliament became known as the "Intolerable Acts"—what point of view on the issue does this name show?*

4. Tell students that many of the Patriot colonial leaders knew that if they were going to get their way with Parliament and

defend the rights of the colonies, they would need to work together, because otherwise each colony was too small to be effective. Some of the colonial leaders decided to get together to discuss the problems they were facing, and the delegates of twelve of the colonies (all but Georgia) met in Philadelphia in 1774 in the First Continental Congress. Ask students to look at their maps and think about why the delegates might have chosen to meet in Philadelphia.

5. Post the **Quotes from the First Continental Congress** (Handout 7B) on the board or overhead for students. Use the quotes to discuss with students the differing opinions of the colonial delegates on the issues of how to relate to Great Britain and one another. For each quote, ask questions such as the following:

   ◆ *What do you think was meant by the quote?*

   ◆ *What are the implications of the statement for the Congress?*

   ◆ *What are the implications of the statement for the future of the colonies?*

   ◆ *How does our knowledge of history and how the colonies came together as one nation affect our interpretation of the statements?*

6. Explain that by the spring of 1775, the Massachusetts colonial assembly had been disbanded by the British government, and the Patriots in Massachusetts were meeting in secret and storing guns and ammunition for what they feared would become an armed conflict with the British. Two of the leaders of the Massachusetts Patriots, John Hancock and Samuel Adams, were continuing to write and make speeches against the actions of the British, and British officials soon moved to arrest them. Distribute copies of the **Map of Boston, Lexington, and Concord** (Handout 7C). Have students look at the map and figure out what spot on their larger map it shows in close-up form. Tell students that on the night of April 18, 1775, British troops stationed in Boston began moving toward Lexington and Concord. They had found out that Hancock and Adams were hiding at a house in Lexington, and they also wanted to seize the store of arms the Americans had at Concord.

7. Give students copies of **Lexington** (Handout 7D), an account of the first shots of the war on Lexington Green from Jonas Clark, the Patriot minister of the village church. Have

students read the account and use **Analyzing Primary Sources** (Handout 7E) to note key ideas from the document. *(Note: The full primary source analysis model, including the second page, is given in this lesson; you may wish to take this opportunity to begin introducing the questions on the second page to students.)* Discuss the document with students, using the analysis sheet and the following questions:

◆ *What was the sequence of events at Lexington Green, according to the document? Describe what you think the scene looked like on that morning.*

◆ *What were the British troops like, as portrayed in the document? Do you think the descriptions are accurate? Why or why not? In what ways does the document show the author's feelings about the British troops?*

◆ *According to the document, who fired first?* (Explain to students that there is some uncertainty about who fired the first shot of the Revolution; some say the British, some say one of the Americans either in the group of militia or from somewhere to the side.) *How would the answer to the question affect how people viewed the incident?*

8. Share with students (or have them read in a secondary source) the events that ensued after the first shots at Lexington. Explain to students that the British proceeded to Concord, but there they were met by a larger group of American militia. The Americans drove the British back at the North Bridge over the Concord River, and the British retreated toward Boston, with militia snipers firing at them most of the way along the road. Refer students to the **Map of Boston, Lexington, and Concord** (Handout 7C).

9. Read with students the excerpt from the Emerson poem **The Shot Heard 'Round the World** (Handout 7F) and ask students what they think was meant by the title phrase. Ask students to think about the implications of the events of April 19, 1775, for the American colonists and for the British. Ask students the following:

◆ *What does hindsight mean?*

◆ *What did Emerson know when he wrote the poem that the militia in Concord did not know?*

Journal

Think about the generalization that an effect can be the result of multiple causes with different degrees of influence. How was the beginning of the war at Lexington and Concord an effect that resulted from multiple causes? How did these different causes influence the effect?

Homework

Finish your persuasive letter about the Boston Tea Party.

Extension

Read Henry Wadsworth Longfellow's poem *Paul Revere's Ride*. Then read accounts of Paul Revere's actions in at least two other sources. How accurate is the poem? What does it leave out? Why do you think these things are left out?

Notes to Teacher

1. This lesson may require more than one class period to complete. You may wish to break the lesson before the discussion of Clark's account of Lexington.

2. Several resources to support the extension activity on the ride of Paul Revere are listed in the resources section at the back of the unit.

3. The Schoolhouse Rock "America Rocks" video and audio cassette/CD include a song called "The Shot Heard 'Round the World" that you may wish to share with students in this lesson or later in the unit; it addresses several key events and names in the Revolution.

Assessment

- ◆ Persuasive writing on the Boston Tea Party
- ◆ Primary source analysis activity
- ◆ Journal responses
- ◆ Participation in discussion

Name_____ Date _____

Map of the 13 Colonies

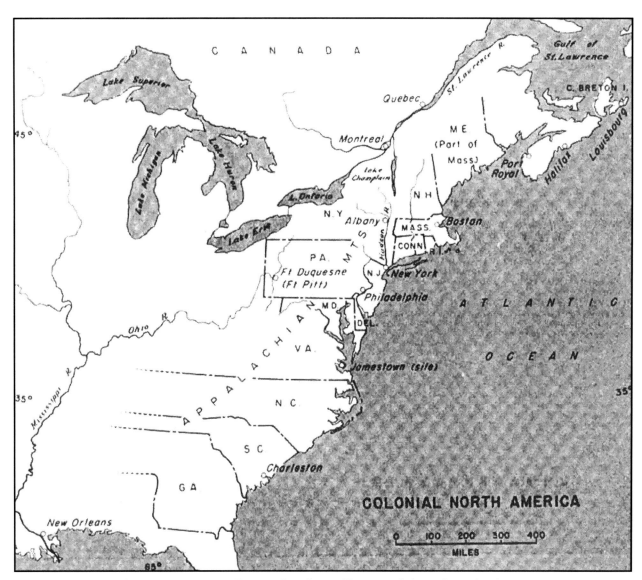

Source: University of Texas PCL Map Collection, *http://www.lib.utexas.edu/maps/histus.html*.

Quotes from the First Continental Congress

"All America is thrown into one mass. Where are your landmarks – your boundaries of colonies? They are all thrown down. The distinctions between Virginians, Pennsylvanians, New Yorkers, and New Englanders are no more. I am not a Virginian, but an American."

—Patrick Henry, speech in Congress, Sept. 6, 1774

"This day convinced me that America will support Massachusetts or perish with her."

—John Adams, diary entry, Sept. 18, 1774

". . . The Colonies hold in abhorrence the idea of being considered independent communities on the British government, and most ardently desire the establishment of a Political Union, not only among themselves, but with the Mother State, upon those principles of safety and freedom which are essential in the constitution of all free governments. . . ."

—Joseph Galloway, proposed Plan of Union,
Sept. 28, 1774 (adoption defeated by one vote)

"Permit us to be as free as yourselves, and we shall ever esteem a union with you to be our greatest glory and our greatest happiness. But if you are determined that your ministers shall wantonly sport with the rights of mankind; if neither the voice of justice, the dictates of law, the principles of the constitution, or the suggestions of humanity, can restrain your hands from shedding human blood in such an impious cause, we must then tell you that we will never submit to be hewers of wood or drawers of water for any ministry or nation in the world."

—from Congress's petition to the king,
accompanying the Declaration of Rights
and Grievances, October 1774

Map of Boston, Lexington, and Concord

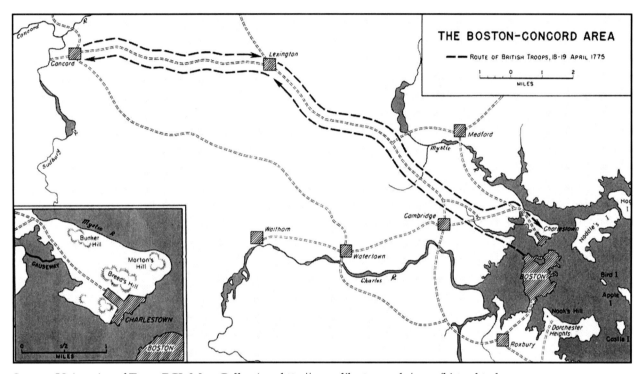

Source: University of Texas PCL Map Collection, *http://www.lib.utexas.edu/maps/histus.html*.

Lexington

(From a sermon by the Reverend Jonas Clark, pastor of the church in Lexington.)

Between the hours of twelve and one, on the morning of the nineteenth of April, we received intelligence, by express, from the Honorable Joseph Warren, Esq., at Boston, "that a large body of the king's troops . . . were embarked in boats from Boston . . . and that it was shrewdly suspected that they were ordered to seize and destroy the stores belonging to the colony, then deposited at Concord" . . .

Upon this intelligence, as also upon information of the conduct of the officers as above-mentioned, the militia of this town were alarmed and ordered to meet on the usual place of parade; not with any design of commencing hostilities upon the king's troops, but to consult what might be done for our own and the people's safety . . .

About half an hour after four o'clock, alarm guns were fired and the drums beat to arms, and the militia were collecting together. Some, to the number of about 50 or 60, or possibly more, were on the parade, others were coming towards it. . . . When within about half a quarter of a mile of the meeting-house, [the British troops] halted, and the command was given to prime and load which being done, they marched on till they came up to the east end of said meeting-house, in sight of our militia. . . .

Immediately upon their appearing so suddenly and so nigh, Capt. Parker, who commanded the militia company, ordered the men to disperse and take care of themselves, and not to fire. Upon this, our men dispersed—but many of them not so speedily as they might have done, not having the most distant idea of such brutal barbarity and more than savage cruelty from the troops of a British king, as they immediately experienced! . . .

The troops shouted aloud, huzza'd, and rushed furiously towards our men . . . Three officers advanced on horseback to the front of the body, and coming within 5 or 6 rods of the militia, one of them cried out, "Ye villains! ye Rebels, disperse!—or words to this effect. One of them said "Lay down your arms!" The second of these officers, about this time, fired a pistol towards the militia as they were dispersing. The foremost, who was within a few yards of our men, brandishing his sword and then pointing towards them, with a loud voice said to the troops, "Fire! By God, fire!"—which was instantly followed by a discharge of arms from the said troops, succeeded by a very heavy and close fire upon our party, dispersing, so long as any of them were within reach. Eight were left dead upon the ground! Ten were wounded. The rest of the company, through divine goodness, were (to a miracle) preserved unhurt in this murderous action! . . .

After the militia company were dispersed and the firing ceased, the troops drew up and formed in a body on the common, fired a volley and gave three huzzas, by way of triumph and as expressive of the joy of victory and glory of conquest!

Source: Bruun and Crosby, *Our Nation's Archive*, pp. 119–120.

Name_____ Date _____ # Handout

Analyzing Primary Sources

Document Title:_____

Establishing a Context and Intent for the Source

> Author:
>
> Time (When was it written)?
>
> Briefly describe the culture of the time and list related events of the time.
>
> Purpose (Why was the document created?)
>
> Audience (Who was the document created for?)

Understanding the Source

> What problems/issues/events does the source address?
>
> What are the main points/ideas/arguments?
>
> What assumptions/values/feelings does the author reflect?
>
> What actions/outcomes does the author expect? From whom?

Authenticity/Reliability (Could the source be invented, edited, or mistranslated? What corroborating evidence do you have about the source? Does the author know enough about the topic to discuss it?)

Representative (How typical is the source of others of the same period? What other information might you need to find this out?)

What could the consequences of this document be? (What would happen if the author's plans were carried out? What could happen to the author when people read this? How might this document affect or change public opinions?)

What were the actual consequences? What really happened as a result of this document?

Short-term

Long-term

What new or different interpretation does this source provide about the historical period?

Handout

The Shot Heard 'Round the World (Excerpt)

By the rude bridge that arched the flood,

Their flag to April's breeze unfurled,

Here once the embattled farmers stood

And fired the shot heard 'round the world.

—by Ralph Waldo Emerson

Settling into War

Curriculum Alignment

Goal 1	Goal 2	Goal 3	Goal 4	Goal 5
X	X	X	X	X

Instructional Purpose

- ◆ To discuss the concept of cause and effect as it applies to the start of the Revolution
- ◆ To trace the chronology of events of the Revolution
- ◆ To outline implications of major events of the Revolution

Materials/Resources

1. Strips of paper
2. Yankee Doodle (Handout 8A)
3. Reasoning about a Situation or Event (Handout 8B)
4. Chronology of War: The North (Handout 8C)
5. Chronology of War: The Middle States (Handout 8D)
6. Chronology of War: The South (Handout 8E)
7. Resources on the Revolution/Internet access

Vocabulary

commander in chief—the supreme commander of a nation's armed forces

parody—a literary, artistic, or musical work that imitates the style of another work or author for ridicule or comic effect

Yankee—term used by British soldiers in the colonial period to ridicule New Englanders, adopted popularly by New Englanders to describe themselves after the battle of Lexington; the term has been used to describe all Americans but also to describe specifically Northerners

📖 Activities

1. Have students take their Boston Tea Party letters and put them together into a page or booklet of "Letters to the Editor." Encourage students to read and discuss one another's letters.

2. Have students work in small groups to create "cause and effect chains" of events they have studied so far. Distribute strips of paper about eight inches long and an inch wide, and also pass out staplers or tape. Have students write "economic conditions after the French and Indian War" on one strip and "battles at Lexington and Concord" on another. Then encourage the students to work with their groups to determine conditions and events that occurred between these two, writing each on a strip, making a loop of the strip, and linking the loops together in a cause-and-effect order. Remind students that given causes can have multiple effects and that given effects can have multiple causes, so each loop might have multiple other loops connected to it.

3. Have the groups share their chains and discuss differences in how the groups interpreted the sequence of events. Ask students to predict what they think the *effects* of the events at Lexington and Concord might have been. *Do you think the events of April 19 were what the British would have expected them to be? Why or why not?*

4. Have students read the different verses provided from **Yankee Doodle** (Handout 8A). Explain to students that the song was originally a British song, used to mock the American soldiers during the French and Indian War (Why?). Tell students that British troops had sung the song on their way to reinforce the soldiers at Lexington on April 19 but that the American troops sang it back to mock the British as the British retreated to Boston after Concord. Ask students to discuss the following questions:

    ◆ *What do the words of this song mean? In what ways does it make fun of the American colonists? What assumptions does it make about them?*

    ◆ *Why do you think the song became so popular among the American troops, if originally it was supposed to be making fun of them?*

    ◆ *Soon after April of 1775, the song was published with the following title: "Yankee Doodle, or The Lexington March." Do you think this was meant to make fun of the British or American troops? Why?*

5. Tell students that in the days and weeks after Lexington and Concord, while militia forces in Massachusetts moved to blockade the roads out of Boston and imprison the British there, patriots in other colonies began to prepare for war. At the same time, the delegates from all thirteen colonies met in Philadelphia starting on May 10 for the Second Continental Congress. (Discuss with students whether they think this was an *effect* of Lexington and Concord. Explain that the meeting had actually been scheduled when the First Continental Congress disbanded the previous year; help students to recognize that the breakout of war did not cause the Congress to meet, although it certainly *affected* what they discussed.)

6. Remind students of the issue they discussed in Lesson 7, that the Continental Congress was a gathering of delegates from colonies that were not otherwise unified in any formal way. Explain that as the Second Continental Congress met, they had to decide whether the events in Massachusetts represented a war for them all to fight, or whether the issue was for Massachusetts or New England only. Explain that the Congress decided by the middle of June, 1775, to adopt the fighting force in Massachusetts and create a Continental Army. Then they had another decision to make: How should the Congress make its decision about who should be commander in chief?

7. Distribute copies of **Reasoning about a Situation or Event** (Handout 8B). Tell students that some of the leading voices in the debate in Congress were three men from Massachusetts: Samuel Adams, who proposed that the troops should be able to elect their own officers; John Hancock, who was president of the Congress and wanted to be the commander in chief himself; and John Adams, who nominated Colonel George Washington from Virginia. Work with students to consider these different options and how the Congress would have responded to them and why, using the questions on the sheet.

8. Explain to students that in the next lesson, they will be learning more about George Washington and the decision of the Congress to make him the leader of the army.

9. Tell students that to help the class get an overall sense of the military chronology of the war, they will be working in groups to learn about major campaigns and to share those with their classmates. Divide the class into three groups. Assign each group one of the **Chronology of War** handouts (Handouts 8C, 8D, 8E) and go over the expectations of the

assignment. Assure students that they will have some class time and resources to complete their work. Allow student groups time to meet and start thinking about their assignment.

Homework

Begin collecting and reading information for your group project.

Extension

1. Many songs of the Revolutionary period included both the original versions and parodies that supported the other side and/or made fun of the original songs. Explore Revolutionary music and make a collection of originals and parodies to share with the class.

2. The term "Yankee" has been used over the history of the United States in many different ways, with slightly different meanings, and including both positive and negative connotations. Explore and outline the history of this term and its various meanings.

Notes to Teacher

1. The group project assigned in this lesson asks students to collect and share information on key battles of the Revolution. The tasks assigned may be expanded or abbreviated as needed based on time and resource availability. Some general resources on the war are listed in the resources section at the back of the unit. The following list of web sites may be helpful in finding out information about the various battles (several are general sites, several are specific to the battles named):

   ◆ General sites:

   http://www.pbs.org/ktca/liberty/index.html

   http://www.historyplace.com/unitedstates/revolution/

   http://www.hillsdale.edu/academics/history/Documents/ War/EMAmRev.htm (has several short primary source documents related to different battles)

   http://theamericanrevolution.org/battles.asp (listing of major battles with details)

- North: *http://www.masshist.org/bh/* (Bunker Hill)

  http://battle1777.saratoga.org/ (from Saratoga Chamber of Commerce)

  http://www.pbs.org/ktca/liberty/chronicle/episode4.html (Saratoga)

- Middle States:

  http://www.pbs.org/ktca/liberty/chronicle/episode3.html (Trenton)

  http://www.barracks.org/barracks/index.html (Trenton)

  http://www.ushistory.org/march/phila/brandywine.htm (Brandywine)

  http://www.brandywine225.com/ (Brandywine)

- South:

  http://www.schistory.org/displays/RevWar/CarolinaDay/battle.html (Sullivan's Island)

  http://www.ccpl.org/ccl/ftmoultrie.html (Sullivan's Island)

  http://www.wilkesnc.org/history/ovta.htm (Kings Mountain)

2. Student projects on the battles of the Revolution should be completed by Lesson 15 for sharing. You may also wish to assign intermediate due dates for parts of the project or to have the groups report out as you work chronologically through the unit to encourage students to learn about the major battles from their classmates as they go. Provide some class time for students to work on their projects over the next few lessons.

Assessment

- Cause and effect chains
- Participation in discussion
- Reasoning chart
- Group project work

Notes

Yankee Doodle

Early version, possibly written by a British army doctor during the French and Indian War:

Brother Ephraim sold his cow
And bought him a commission
And then he went to Canada
To fight for the nation;
But when Ephraim,
he came home
He proved an arrant coward,
He wouldn't fight the
Frenchmen there
For fear of being devoured.

Sheep's head and vinegar
Buttermilk and tansy
Boston is a Yankee town,
Sing "Hey, doodle dandy!"

from a British version sung in April 1775:

Yankee Doodle came to town,
For to buy a firelock,
We will tar and feather him,
And so will we John Hancock.

from a standard early version:

Father and I went down to camp
Along with Captain Goodwin
And there we saw the men and boys
As thick as hasty puddin'.

from an early American version making fun of Washington:

And there was Captain Washington
And gentle folks about him;
They say he's grown so tarnal proud
He will not ride without them.

from an American version preferred by the American soldiers:

Yankee Doodle is the tune
That we all delight in;
It suits for feasts,
it suits for fun,
And just as well for fightin'.

Sources: McNeil and McNeil, *Colonial and Revolution Songbook,* pp. 42–43;
Fleming, *Liberty! The American Revolution,* p. 125.

Reasoning about a Situation or Event

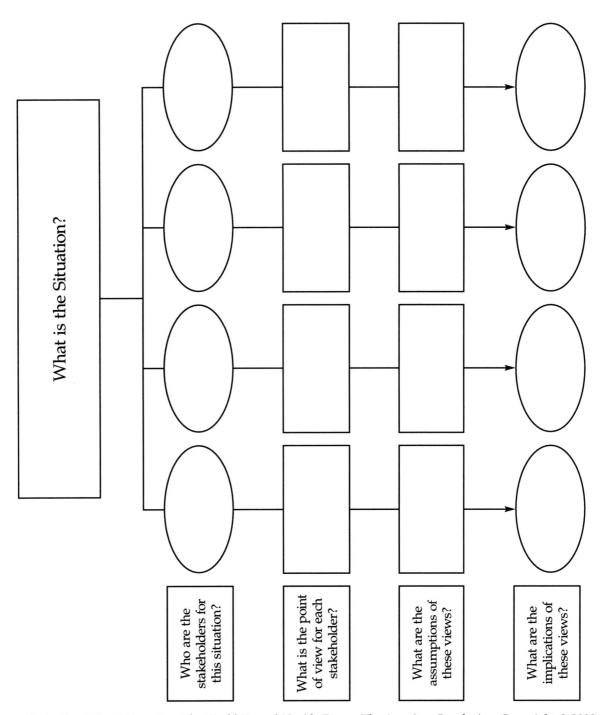

What is the Situation?

Who are the stakeholders for this situation?

What is the point of view for each stakeholder?

What are the assumptions of these views?

What are the implications of these views?

Chronology of War: The North

Your group will be helping your classmates to understand some of the major military events of the Revolutionary War in the *North*. Specifically, your group will be finding out about the following battles:

- Bunker Hill

- Saratoga

When you are researching the battles, you will need to read about the battles themselves and also about the time *leading up to* each battle and *following* each battle to help you understand the battles thoroughly. Use the questions below to help you organize your research:

- When did this battle take place? What were some important events *leading up to* this battle?

- Why did the battle occur where it did? Why was the area important to the British, and why was it important to the Americans?

- Who were the major military leaders on both sides?

- What were some important features or events of the battle?

- Who won? Was it a *decisive* victory?

- What were the effects of the battle for the Americans? What were the effects of the battle for the British?

After you have collected your information, you will put together a poster to share with the class. On your poster, you will need to include the following pieces:

- A **map** of your region of the colonies, with your battle locations marked and lines to show the movement of British and American troops to the battles (see your map of Boston, Lexington, and Concord for an example).

- A **timeline** of major military events in your region from the time of your first battle to the time of your second battle.

- A **description** of each battle, including some of the details you found to answer the questions above. Each description should be about one page long.

- A **Hamburger Model** paragraph discussing why each of your battles was important in the Revolution.

- At least one **quote** about each battle from a primary source document from the time.

Group members: Important Due Dates:

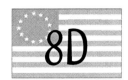

Chronology of War:
The Middle States

Your group will be helping your classmates to understand some of the major military events of the Revolutionary War in the *Middle States*. Specifically, your group will be finding out about the following battles:

- ◆ Trenton

- ◆ Brandywine

When you are researching the battles, you will need to read about the battles themselves and also about the time *leading up to* each battle and *following* each battle to help you understand the battles thoroughly. Use the questions below to help you organize your research:

- ◆ When did this battle take place? What were some important events *leading up to* this battle?

- ◆ Why did the battle occur where it did? Why was the area important to the British, and why was it important to the Americans?

- ◆ Who were the major military leaders on both sides?

- ◆ What were some important features or events of the battle?

- ◆ Who won? Was it a *decisive* victory?

- ◆ What were the effects of the battle for the Americans? What were the effects of the battle for the British?

After you have collected your information, you will put together a poster to share with the class. On your poster, you will need to include the following pieces:

- A **map** of your region of the colonies, with your battle locations marked and lines to show the movement of British and American troops to the battles (see your map of Boston, Lexington, and Concord for an example).

- A **timeline** of major military events in your region from the time of your first battle to the time of your second battle.

- A **description** of each battle, including some of the details you found to answer the questions above. Each description should be about one page long.

- A **Hamburger Model** paragraph discussing why each of your battles was important in the Revolution.

- At least one **quote** about each battle from a primary source document from the time.

Group members: Important Due Dates:

Chronology of War: The South

Your group will be helping your classmates to understand some of the major military events of the Revolutionary War in the *South*. Specifically, your group will be finding out about the following battles:

◆ Sullivan's Island

◆ Kings Mountain

When you are researching the battles, you will need to read about the battles themselves and also about the time *leading up to* each battle and *following* each battle to help you understand the battles thoroughly. Use the questions below to help you organize your research:

◆ When did this battle take place? What were some important events *leading up to* this battle?

◆ Why did the battle occur where it did? Why was the area important to the British, and why was it important to the Americans?

◆ Who were the major military leaders on both sides?

◆ What were some important features or events of the battle?

◆ Who won? Was it a *decisive* victory?

◆ What were the effects of the battle for the Americans? What were the effects of the battle for the British?

After you have collected your information, you will put together a poster to share with the class. On your poster, you will need to include the following pieces:

- A **map** of your region of the colonies, with your battle locations marked and lines to show the movement of British and American troops to the battles (see your map of Boston, Lexington, and Concord for an example).

- A **timeline** of major military events in your region from the time of your first battle to the time of your second battle.

- A **description** of each battle, including some of the details you found to answer the questions above. Each description should be about one page long.

- A **Hamburger Model** paragraph discussing why each of your battles was important in the Revolution.

- At least one **quote** about each battle from a primary source document from the time.

Group members: Important Due Dates:

Leadership in the Revolutionary Era

Curriculum Alignment

Goal 1	Goal 2	Goal 3	Goal 4	Goal 5
	X		X	X

Instructional Purpose

- ◆ To explore leadership in the Revolutionary period
- ◆ To analyze the effects of individuals on events of the time
- ◆ To read and analyze primary source documents

Materials/Resources

1. Washington's Response to Congress (Handout 9A)
2. Washington's Letter to his Wife Martha (Handout 9B)
3. Analyzing Primary Sources (Handout 9C)
4. Biography Outline (Handout 9D)
5. Biography Subjects (Handout 9E)

Vocabulary

unanimous—having the complete agreement of all members of a group

Activities

1. Remind students of their discussion in the previous lesson about the decision in the Continental Congress to appoint George Washington as commander in chief of the Continental Army. Review with students the understanding that although Washington had military experience, the larger reason for his selection was that he was a respected Virginian, and that Congress hoped to unify the colonies by putting a Virginian in command of an army that was, for the moment, mainly fighting in New England. Tell students that although some members of Congress discussed other options (as students discussed in the previous lesson), when it came to a vote, Washington was selected unanimously.

2. Divide the class in half. Give one half of the class **Washington's Response to Congress** (Handout 9A) and the other half **Washington's Letter to his Wife Martha** (Handout 9B), and give all students copies of **Analyzing Primary Sources** (Handout 9C). Allow students to work in groups within their half of the class to read their documents and complete the analysis sheets.

3. Then redivide the class into pairs so that each pair has one student who read the response to Congress and one who read the letter. In their pairs, students should briefly summarize what they read and discussed in their first group. Then they should discuss the following questions:

   ◆ *In what ways are the two documents alike? In what ways are they different? Why?*

   ◆ *What have you learned about George Washington from these documents? What do they show about his character, his thoughts, and his values? What do they show about George Washington as a leader?*

   ◆ *How do you think the audiences of the two documents would have responded?*

4. Tell students that when we study history, we often divide our attention between the experiences of large groups of people, or the ordinary people in society, and the actions and experiences of particular people who are memorable for one reason or another. Some of the most well-known figures in American history are remembered for their actions during the Revolutionary era. Tell students that they will be doing a biography project in which they find out about some of these famous figures of the Revolutionary period.

5. Introduce **Biography Outline** (Handout 9D) and **Biography Subjects** (Handout 9E) and go over with students. Explain that their purpose in completing the biography assignment will be to help them understand why we remember these individuals from their influence during the Revolutionary period. Students should prepare the biography to be completed before Lesson 19.

Journal

What do you think are the characteristics that make a good leader? Describe someone you know who you think is a good leader.

Homework

Begin gathering information on the subject of your biography project.

Note to Teacher

The list of individuals for the biography project is by no means an exhaustive list of key figures of the period. Other individuals may be added to the list for student choice as desired.

Assessment

- ◆ Primary source analysis
- ◆ Journal response
- ◆ Biography project

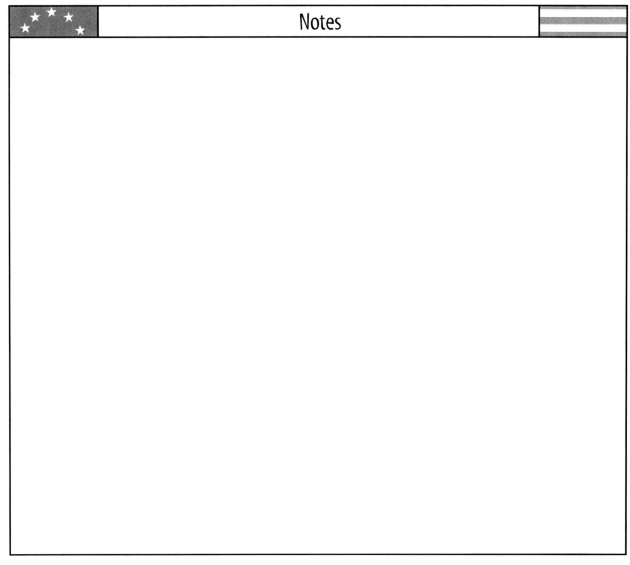

Notes

Washington's Response to Congress

June 16, 1775

Mr. President:

Tho' I am truly sensible of the high Honour done me in this Appointment, yet I feel great distress from a consciousness that my abilities and Military experience may not be equal to the extensive and important Trust: However, as the Congress desire it I will enter upon the momentous duty, and exert every power I Possess In their service and for the Support of the glorious Cause: I beg they will accept my most cordial thanks for this distinguished testimony of their Approbation.

But lest some unlucky event should happen unfavourable to my reputation, I beg it may be remembered by every Gentleman in the room, that I this day declare with the utmost sincerity, I do not think myself equal to the Command I am honoured with.

As to pay, Sir, I beg leave to Assure the Congress that as no pecuniary consideration could have tempted me to have accepted this Arduous employment at the expence of my domestic ease and happiness I do not wish to make any profit from it: I will keep an exact Account of my expences; those I doubt not they will discharge and that is all I desire.

Source: Bruun and Crosby, *Our Nation's Archive*, pp. 121–122.

Washington's Letter to his Wife Martha

June 18, 1775

My Dearest:

I am now set down to write you on a subject which fills me with inexpressible concern, and this concern is greatly aggravated and increased, when I reflect upon the uneasiness I know it will cause you. It has been determined in Congress, that the whole army raised for the defence of the American cause shall be put under my care, and that it is necessary for me to proceed immediately to Boston to take command of it.

You may believe me, my dear Patcy, when I assure you, in the most solemn manner, that, so far from seeking this appointment, I have used every endeavor in my power to avoid it, not only from my unwillingness to part with you and the family, but from a consciousness of its being a trust too great for my capacity, and that I should enjoy more real happiness in one month with you at home than I have the most distant prospect of finding abroad, if my stay were to be seven times seven years. But as it has been a kind of destiny that has thrown me upon this service, I shall hope that my undertaking it is designed to answer some good purpose. . . .

It was utterly out of my power to refuse the appointment, without exposing my character to such censures, as would have reflected dishonor upon myself, and given pain to my friends. This, I am sure, could not, and ought not, to be pleasing to you, and must have lessened me considerably in my own esteem. I shall rely, therefore, confidently on that Providence which has heretofore preserved and been bountiful to me, not doubting but that I shall return safe to you in the fall. I shall feel no pain from the toil or the danger of the campaign; my unhappiness will flow from the uneasiness I know you will feel from being left alone. I therefore beg, that you will summon your whole fortitude, and pass your time as agreeably as possible. Nothing will give me so much sincere satisfaction as to hear this, and to hear it from your own pen. . . .

Source: Bruun and Crosby, *Our Nation's Archive,* p. 122.

Name_____ Date _____

Analyzing Primary Sources

Document Title:_____

Establishing a Context and Intent for the Source

Author:

Time (When was it written)?

Briefly describe the culture of the time and list related events of the time.

Purpose (Why was the document created?)

Audience (Who was the document created for?)

Understanding the Source

What problems/issues/events does the source address?

What are the main points/ideas/arguments?

What assumptions/values/feelings does the author reflect?

What actions/outcomes does the author expect? From whom?

Authenticity/Reliability (Could the source be invented, edited, or mistranslated? What corroborating evidence do you have about the source? Does the author know enough about the topic to discuss it?)

Representative (How typical is the source of others of the same period? What other information might you need to find this out?)

What could the consequences of this document be? (What would happen if the author's plans were carried out? What could happen to the author when people read this? How might this document affect or change public opinions?)

What were the actual consequences? What really happened as a result of this document?

Short-term

Long-term

What new or different interpretation does this source provide about the historical period?

Biography Outline

You will be researching the life of one person who had a prominent influence during the Revolutionary period. Your main goal is to discover *how this person influenced events of the time and how this person's life was influenced by the events.* To meet this goal, you will need to find out about the person's life before, during, and after the Revolution. Some guiding questions to help you are listed below.

- What are the person's "vital statistics"? *(dates of birth and death, where he or she lived, what kind of education, whether he or she married and had children)*

- What were the important influences on this person's life?

- What was this person's job or role before the Revolution?

- What was this person's role during the Revolutionary period (1765–1783)?

- What issues were important to this person? What point of view did he or she take on those issues?

- What do you think were the most important decisions this person had to make? What influenced the decisions?

- Why was this person significant to the history of the Revolution?

- What effects did the Revolution have on this person's life? How did his or her life change?

Once you have completed your research, you will prepare a written product and a presentation to share with the class in a "Gallery of Greats." When you prepare your project to share with the class, you will include the following pieces:

1. A timeline of important events in the person's life

2. An essay discussing why this person was an important figure in the Revolutionary period

3. A paragraph discussing how the events of the Revolution caused change in the person's life

4. A visual representing something important about the person's life; this may be an object you bring in or some kind of picture or model you prepare

5. Two quotes from primary sources written by or about the person; choose quotes that you think show something important about the person's actions or personality

Project due date:

Name_____ Date _____

Biography Subjects

The following list includes many different people who were prominent figures during the Revolutionary period. You may choose one of these people for your biography or another individual approved by the teacher.

Abigail Adams	Marquis de Lafayette
John Adams	Richard Henry Lee
Samuel Adams	Francis Marion
Benedict Arnold	Joseph Plumb Martin
Gen. John Burgoyne	George Mason
Gen. Henry Clinton	Thomas Paine
Lord Cornwallis	Israel Putnam
John Dickinson	Paul Revere
Benjamin Franklin	Count de Rochambeau
George III	Charles Townshend
Nathaniel Greene	Friedrich Wilhelm von Steuben
John Hancock	Joseph Warren
Mary Ludwig Hays	Mercy Warren
Patrick Henry	George Washington
William Howe	Martha Washington
Thomas Jefferson	Phyllis Wheatley
John Paul Jones	George Wythe

Independence?

Lesson 10

Curriculum Alignment

Goal 1	Goal 2	Goal 3	Goal 4	Goal 5
X	X		X	X

Instructional Purpose

- ◆ To identify potential implications of the Continental Congress's decision to declare independence
- ◆ To read and analyze documents that influenced the decision to declare independence
- ◆ To trace the chronology of the decision for independence

Materials/Resources

1. Olive Branch Petition (Handout 10A)
2. Excerpts from *Common Sense* (Handout 10B)
3. Analyzing Primary Sources (Handout 10C)
4. Reasoning Web (Handout 10D)

Vocabulary

independence—for a country, the condition of being free and self-governing, not governed by a foreign power

olive branch—an offer of peace or goodwill, based on traditional symbolism of the branch of the olive tree representing peace

petition—a formal document making a request of a person or group in authority; often requesting a right or benefit

radical—favoring major or revolutionary changes in current practices, conditions, or institutions

Activities

1. Have students begin the lesson by writing a response to the following question in their journals: *Why do we celebrate on the Fourth of July? What event does that date commemorate?* Invite students to share their responses, and tell students that over the next few lessons they will be discussing the events that led to the signing of the Declaration of Independence in July of 1776.

2. Explain to students that even though the Continental Congress had voted to establish an army and put George Washington at the head of it, many members of the Congress (and people of the colonies) were still quite hopeful of a reconciliation with Great Britain, and the patriots who were promoting the establishment of an independent country were still seen as radicals. Have students read the **Olive Branch Petition** (Handout 10A), passed in Congress in July 1775, and discuss the following questions, related to the elements of reasoning:

   ◆ *What is an olive branch? Why is that title given to the petition?*

   ◆ *What point of view does the petition express about the conflict going on between the American colonists and the British? How do you know?*

   ◆ *What assumptions does the petition make about what the relationship between Britain and the colonies should be?*

   ◆ *What inferences or conclusions can we draw from the petition about what the Continental Congress felt at this point about the idea of independence from Britain? What specific parts of the document support the inferences?*

3. Tell students that despite these feelings about the possibility of reconciliation, the hostilities continued to escalate, both on the battlefields of the war and in the written communications between Congress and the British. Some of the more radical members of Congress, including John Adams and Benjamin Franklin, began talking more of independence and drafting documents that spoke of the idea. One of the most influential documents expressing this point of view was a pamphlet written by an Englishman who had moved to the American colonies, Thomas Paine. Paine wrote a pamphlet called *Common Sense* that expressed the position that it was time for

the colonies and Britain to part ways. Have students read **Excerpts from *Common Sense*** (Handout 10B) and work in small groups to complete **Analyzing Primary Sources** (Handout 10C). Tell students that *Common Sense* was widely read across the colonies and helped to stir support for declaring independence.

4. Explain to students that by the spring of 1776, the Congress was debating the idea of declaring independence from Great Britain. Distribute copies of the **Reasoning Web** (Handout 10D) and explain that for homework and in the next lesson, students will be using this sheet to help them organize their thinking about the issue under debate in the Continental Congress. Remind students that they have seen some of these elements in other activities and discussions, and explain that they actually use all of these elements in trying to reason about a problem or issue. Ask students to state the issue facing Congress in 1776, using a question form (e.g., *Should the colonies declare their independence from Great Britain?*) and to write their question into the **issue** bubble. Then tell students that for homework they should think about *why* Congress was debating the issue and *what different points of view* there were on the issue; have them fill in the **purpose** and **point of view** bubbles with their responses.

Journal

Think about the generalization that causes may have predictable and unpredictable effects. How do you think this idea affected the thoughts of the members of Congress in the spring of 1776?

Homework

Fill in the purpose and point of view bubbles on your Reasoning Web.

Extension

John Adams wrote many letters to his wife Abigail while he was in Philadelphia with the Continental Congress. Locate and read some of his letters from the months before the Declaration of Independence and write a description of what you think the Congress's debates were like, based on his comments.

Assessment

- Primary source analysis
- Journal responses
- Participation in discussion

Notes

10A

Olive Branch Petition

July 8, 1775

To the King's Most Excellent Majesty.

MOST GRACIOUS SOVEREIGN:

At the conclusion . . . of the late war, the most glorious and advantageous that ever had been carried on by British arms, your loyal Colonists having contributed to its success by such repeated and strenuous exertions as frequently procured them the distinguished approbation of your Majesty, of the late King, and of Parliament, doubted not but that they should be permitted, with the rest of the Empire, to share in the blessings of peace, and the emoluments of victory and conquest. . . .

[But] they were alarmed by a new system of statutes and regulations adopted for the administration of the Colonies, that filled their minds with the most painful fears and jealousies; and, to their inexpressible astonishment, perceived the danger of a foreign quarrel quickly succeeded by domestic danger, in their judgment of a more dreadful kind. . . .

Your Majesty's Ministers, persevering in their measures, and proceeding to open hostilities for enforcing them, have compelled us to arm in our own defence, and have engaged us in a controversy so peculiarly abhorrent to the affections of your still faithful Colonists, that when we consider whom we must oppose in this contest, and if it continues, what may be the consequences, our own particular misfortunes are accounted by us only as parts of our distress. . . .

Attached to your Majesty's person, family, and Government, with all devotion that principle and affection can inspire; connected with Great Britain by the strongest ties that can unite societies, and deploring every event that tends in any degree to weaken them, we solemnly assure your Majesty, that we not only most ardently desire the former harmony between her and these Colonies may be restored, but that a concord may be established between them upon so firm a basis as to perpetuate its blessings, uninterrupted by any future dissensions, to succeeding generations in both countries. . . .

We beg further leave to assure your Majesty, that notwithstanding the sufferings of your loyal Colonists during the course of this present controversy, our breasts retain too tender a regard for the kingdom from which we derive our origin, to request such a reconciliation as might, in any manner, be inconsistent with her dignity or welfare. . . . The apprehensions that now oppress our hearts with unspeakable grief, being once removed, your Majesty will find our faithful subject on this Continent ready and willing at all times, as they have ever been with their lives and fortunes, to assert and maintain the rights and interests of your Majesty, and of our Mother Country. . . .

Excerpts from *Common Sense*

Common Sense by Thomas Paine, Philadelphia, Feb. 14, 1776.

. . . I have heard it asserted by some, that as America hath flourished under her former connection with Great Britain, that the same connection is necessary towards her future happiness, and will always have the same effect. . . . We may as well assert, that because a child has thrived upon milk, that it is never to have meat; or that the first twenty years of our lives is to become a precedent for the next twenty. But even this is admitting more than is true, for I answer roundly, that America would have flourished as much, and probably much more, had no European power had any thing to do with her. The commerce by which she hath enriched herself are the necessaries of life, and will always have a market while eating is the custom of Europe. . . .

But Britain is the parent country, say some. Then the more shame upon her conduct. Even brutes do not devour their young; nor savages make war upon their families; wherefore the assertion, if true, turns to her reproach; but it happens not to be true, or only partly so . . . Europe, and not England, is the parent country of America. This new world hath been the asylum for the persecuted lovers of civil and religious liberty from every Part of Europe. . . .

I challenge the warmest advocate for reconciliation to show a single advantage that this continent can reap, by being connected with Great Britain. I repeat the challenge, not a single advantage is derived. Our corn will fetch its price in any market in Europe, and our imported goods must be paid for, buy them where we will.

But the injuries and disadvantages we sustain by that connection are without number; and our duty to mankind at large, as well as to ourselves, instruct us to renounce the alliance: Because, any submission to, or dependance on Great Britain, tends directly to involve this continent in European wars and quarrels; and sets us at variance with nations, who would otherwise seek our friendship, and against whom, we have neither anger nor complaint. As Europe is our market for trade, we ought to form no partial connection with any part of it. . . .

As to government matters, it is not in the powers of Britain to do this continent justice: The business of it will soon be too weighty, and intricate, to be managed with any tolerable degree of convenience, by a power, so distant from us, and so very ignorant of us; for if they cannot conquer us, they cannot govern us. To be always running three or four thousand miles with a tale or a petition, waiting four or five months for an answer, which when obtained requires five or six more to explain it in, will in a few years be looked upon as folly and childishness—there was a time when it was proper, and there is a proper time for it to cease.

Small islands not capable of protecting themselves are the proper objects for kingdoms to take under their care; but there is something very absurd in supposing a continent to be perpetually governed by an island. In no instance hath nature made the satellite larger than its primary planet, and as England and America, with respect to each Other, reverses the common order of nature, it is evident they belong to different systems: England to Europe—America to itself. . . .

A government of our own is our natural right: And when a man seriously reflects on the precariousness of human affairs, he will become convinced, that it is in finitely wiser and safer, to form a constitution of our own in a cool deliberate manner, while we have it in our power, than to trust such an interesting event to time and chance. . . .

However strange it may appear to some, or however unwilling they may be to think so, matters not, but many strong and striking reasons may be given, to show, that nothing can settle our affairs so expeditiously as an open and determined declaration for independence. . . . Under our present denomination of British subjects we can neither be received nor heard abroad: The custom of all courts is against us, and will be so, until, by an independence, we take rank with other nations.

Analyzing Primary Sources

Document Title:_____

Establishing a Context and Intent for the Source

Author:

Time (When was it written)?

Briefly describe the culture of the time and list related events of the time.

Purpose (Why was the document created?)

Audience (Who was the document created for?)

Understanding the Source

What problems/issues/events does the source address?

What are the main points/ideas/arguments?

What assumptions/values/feelings does the author reflect?

What actions/outcomes does the author expect? From whom?

Authenticity/Reliability (Could the source be invented, edited, or mistranslated? What corroborating evidence do you have about the source? Does the author know enough about the topic to discuss it?)

Representative (How typical is the source of others of the same period? What other information might you need to find this out?)

What could the consequences of this document be? (What would happen if the author's plans were carried out? What could happen to the author when people read this? How might this document affect or change public opinions?)

What were the actual consequences? What really happened as a result of this document?

Short-term

Long-term

What new or different interpretation does this source provide about the historical period?

Name_____ Date _____

Reasoning Web

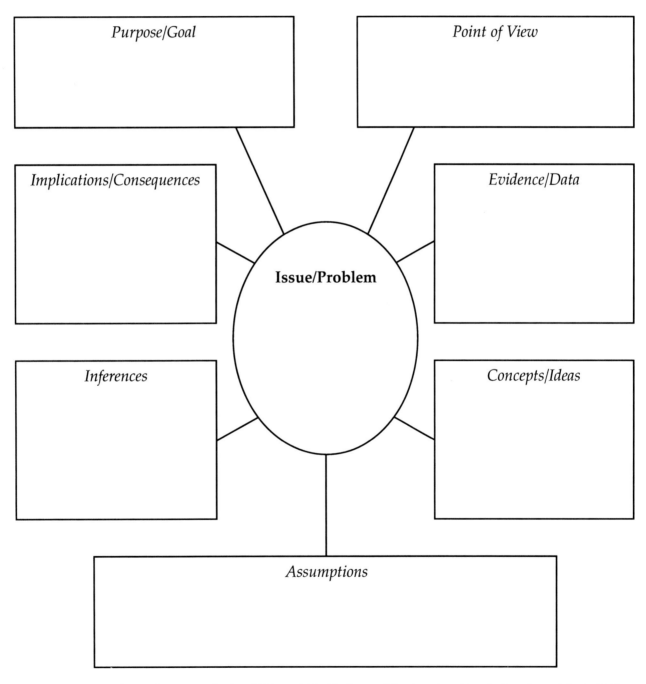

Life, Liberty, and the Pursuit of Happiness

Lesson 11

Curriculum Alignment

Goal 1	Goal 2	Goal 3	Goal 4	Goal 5
	X		X	X

Instructional Purpose

- ◆ To trace the process of the Continental Congress's development of the Declaration of Independence
- ◆ To use the elements of reasoning to analyze issues
- ◆ To develop understanding of key concepts in political theory

Materials/Resources

1. Reasoning Web (Handout 10D from previous lesson)
2. Treatise on Government (Handout 11A)
3. Opening of the Declaration (Handout 11B)
4. Philosophical Connections (Handout 11C)

Vocabulary

declaration—a formal announcement or statement, either written or oral

liberty—freedom from restriction or control; the right to act, believe, and express oneself according to one's own choosing

philosopher—a scholar whose focus is inquiry into reality through logical reasoning; one who strives to achieve and share wisdom

self-evident—requiring no proof, explanation, or reasoning

treatise—a systematic argument in writing on a subject, usually an extensive document

unalienable—describing things not to be separated or taken away

Activities

1. Have students share their responses to the purpose and point of view bubbles on the **Reasoning Web** (Handout 10D) from their homework. Work with students to use the web to continue to discuss the independence issue, using the outline below to clarify the elements on the web (elements do not have to be addressed in any particular order):

   ◆ When we have identified different points of view, we need to consider the **assumptions** that are behind them. Remind students of how they have discussed assumptions when using the **Reasoning about a Situation or Event** chart. Ask the following questions:

      —*What assumptions about government does the point of view supporting independence show? What assumptions about government does the point of view opposing independence show?*

      —*What assumptions was Congress making about the British? The king? What assumptions was Congress making about the colonies?*

   ◆ Explain to students that in order to understand an issue deeply, we need to think about the key ideas and **concepts** that are shaping the issue. Some examples of concepts are freedom, friendship, and responsibility.

      —*What are some of the big ideas Congress was thinking about? How does this issue relate to the idea of **government**? How does it relate to the idea of **liberty**?*

   ◆ Ask students to look at the **evidence** bubble on the web. *What is evidence and why is it important in answering a question?* (It is proof/information/facts/experiences that tell you something about the question; you need it to help you decide the right thing to do, you need it to help convince other people to agree with you.) In reasoning, we need to make sure our evidence is accurate and to look at evidence on both sides of the issue. Ask the following questions:

      —*What sources of evidence do you think Congress was using to support the different points of view?*

      —*What evidence from the documents and events we have studied so far do you think supports the different points of view?*

      —*What other evidence do you think would help with the issue?*

◆ Tell students that based on an understanding of concepts and a review of the evidence, people draw conclusions or **inferences.** Inferences are small steps we take in our mind about the evidence we have to help us answer our question. They can be strong inferences if they are well-thought-out and based on solid evidence, or they can be weak inferences if they are based on weak evidence or if they rely on assumptions more than on the actual evidence. Ask the following:

—*What are some of the inferences that were being made based on the events of 1775-1776? In the Olive Branch Petition, what inferences did Congress make about the role of the king, the Ministers, and the colonies in recent events? What evidence did they use for their inferences?*

—*In August 1775, the king declared the colonies to be in a state of rebellion. What inferences could Congress make about the relationship between Britain and the colonies based on this declaration?*

◆ Point out the bubble for **implications and consequences** and tell students that in reasoning, we have to consider possible outcomes of our decisions to follow through on one point of view or another. We need to think about *what or who will be affected by our decisions* and *what other events might occur as a consequence.* Ask students to think about the following:

—*What were possible implications of declaring independence for Congress? For the colonists in general? For the army?*

—*What were possible implications of declaring independence for Great Britain?*

—*What were possible implications of **not** declaring independence?*

2. Tell students that the Congress, along with Thomas Paine and other thinkers of the time, were heavily influenced in their ideas by several different political philosophers of the seventeenth and eighteenth century, including the seventeenth century English philosopher John Locke. Explain that many of these philosophers were exploring ideas of the purpose of government, why government is necessary, and what types of relationships between a government and a society are most effective or appropriate.

3. Ask students to think about the differences between doing something on their own, like making a decision about what to read or watch on TV or what to play, and doing something in a group with other people. *Why is it different when you are deciding what to do when you have a group of seven or eight people than when you are by yourself or with one friend? In what ways do different rules apply to the activities we do at home on our own or on the playground?* Tell students that political philosophers of the eighteenth century wrote a lot about people's *natural rights*. They discussed the differences between how people could behave in nature (just naturally without the influence of other people, rules, or government) and how people needed to behave in society. *What might some of those differences have been?*

4. Distribute copies of **Treatise on Government** (Handout 11A). Explain that this is an excerpt from a longer work by John Locke in which he discussed his ideas on what government should be like. Ask students the following questions to help them understand the excerpt:

   ◆ *When Locke talks about "legislative power established by consent in the common wealth," what does he mean? For a legislature (like Congress or Parliament) to make laws by consent, what does that mean? How does that idea relate to the colonists' views on Parliament's taxation without representation?*

   ◆ *Why does Locke say a government is important for keeping property safe? Why is property not safe in a state of nature? In a state of nature, why are all people kings?*

5. Return to the Reasoning Web and ask students if they can make any additions to their webs based on reading Locke. Ask students specifically how reading Locke influences their responses to the bubbles for *concepts, assumptions,* and *implications*.

6. Distribute copies of the **Opening of the Declaration** (Handout 11B). Explain that this is part of the opening section of the Declaration of Independence, which they will read fully in the next lesson, but that this section demonstrates how the Congress was reflecting Locke's ideas in declaring themselves free of British rule. Give students copies of **Philosophical Connections** (Handout 11C) and ask them to work in groups to complete the chart, filling in specific quotations from the two documents addressing the key ideas.

7. Review the chart with students. Ask them what similarities as well as differences they noticed between the two documents. *If Locke referred to life, liberty, and property as the key rights of man, why do you think the Declaration uses life, liberty, and the pursuit of happiness? What does this comparison indicate about the intended meaning of the pursuit of happiness?*

8. Tell students that the section of the Declaration that follows what they read in this lesson discusses the idea that if a government does not support the ideals indicated, then the people have a right to dissolve their connections with that government, thus the basis for "declaring independence." In the next lesson they will learn more about this and read the Declaration in its entirety.

Extension

Read more of Locke's *Second Treatise on Government*. Where else do you see the influence of his ideas in the Declaration of Independence?

Note to Teacher

This lesson addresses complex philosophical issues, but a brief introduction to them will enrich students' understanding of the Declaration of Independence and the events that followed it. Some advanced students may also be introduced to longer segments of Locke's treatise. One source for more information on John Locke is the following site: *http://www.johnlocke.org/whowasjl.html.* A search on "Second Treatise on Government" or "John Locke" will also yield other sources of information.

Assessment

♦ Reasoning and connections charts
♦ Participation in discussion

Treatise on Government

The natural liberty of man is to be free from any superior power on earth and not to be under the will or legislative authority of man, but to have only the law of nature for his rule. The liberty of man, in society, is to be under no other legislative power but that established by consent in the commonwealth. . . . Freedom then is not . . . a liberty for everyone to do what he likes, to live as he pleases and not to be tied by any laws: but freedom of men under government is to have a standing rule to live by, common to everyone of that society, and made by the legislative power erected in it; . . . and not to be subject to the inconstant, uncertain, unknown, arbitrary will of another man. . . .

If man in the state of nature be so free . . . why will he part with his freedom? Why will he give up this empire and subject himself to the dominion and control of any other power? To which 'tis obvious to answer, that though in the state of nature he hath such a right, yet the enjoyment of it is very uncertain and constantly exposed to the invasion of others. For all being kings as much as he . . . , the enjoyment of the property he has in this state is very unsafe, very unsecure. This makes him willing to quit a condition which, however free, is full of fears and continual dangers. . . . He seeks out and is willing to join in society with others who are already united, or have a mind to unite, for the mutual preservation of their lives, liberties and estates, which I call by the general name, property.

Source: Locke, *Second Treatise on Government.*

Opening of the Declaration

When in the course of human events, it becomes necessary for one people to dissolve the political bands which have connected them with another, and to assume among the powers of the earth, the separate and equal station to which the laws of Nature and of Nature's God entitle them, a decent respect to the opinions of mankind requires that they should declare the causes which impel them to the separation.

We hold these truths to be self-evident, that all men are created equal, that they are endowed by their Creator with certain unalienable rights, that among these are life, liberty, and the pursuit of happiness. That to secure these rights, governments are instituted among men, deriving their just powers from the consent of the governed. . . .

Philosophical Connections

	Locke	Declaration
Laws of nature		
Basis of legislative or government authority		
Rights of man		

The Declaration
of Independence

Curriculum Alignment

Goal 1	Goal 2	Goal 3	Goal 4	Goal 5
	X		X	X

 Instructional Purpose

- ◆ To trace the process of the Continental Congress's development of the Declaration of Independence
- ◆ To analyze the points of view and evidence expressed in the Declaration of Independence
- ◆ To analyze the implications of the Declaration of Independence for the American colonies

 Materials/Resources

1. Resolutions from Virginia (Handout 12A)
2. Declaration of Independence (Handout 12B)
3. Analyzing Primary Sources (Handout 12C)
4. Standards of Reasoning (Handout 12D)
5. July 3 Letter (Handout 12E)

 Vocabulary

confederation—a group of states or nations united for a common purpose

state—the political organization of a group of people usually occupying a given territory; may be a sovereign government or one of a group that together form a nation with a federal government

 Activities

1. Explain that in order for the Second Continental Congress to decide to declare independence, first one of the colonial assemblies had to issue a resolution, because the delegates to Congress represented their colonial assemblies. The official resolution introduced to Congress came from Richard Henry Lee of Virginia. Share with students the **Resolutions from Virginia** (Handout 12A) and ask the following questions (you may wish to have

students read the resolutions independently or just put the document on the overhead for discussion):

♦ *What was the purpose of the Virginia resolutions?*

♦ *What assumptions do the resolutions suggest about what the connections among the colonies should be in the future?*

2. Explain to students that while some of the delegates conferred with their legislatures about the resolution and whether or not to adopt it, Congress appointed a committee to draft a declaration of independence that could be voted on if the Virginia resolutions passed. This committee included Roger Sherman of Connecticut, Robert Livingston of New York, Benjamin Franklin of Pennsylvania, John Adams of Massachusetts, and Thomas Jefferson of Virginia. *(Who was the main author of the Declaration from this committee?)* Tell students that on July 1 and 2, the Congress again debated on Lee's resolutions and finally passed them on July 2 with 12 colonies supporting them and one (New York) abstaining. So the actual decision to declare independence was on July 2, not July 4! Ask students why they think we celebrate Independence Day on July 4 instead.

3. Ask students why when we write, we often have to reread and revise our writing. What reasons might we have for making changes to our writing? Then ask students to think of group projects they have done, in which they may have an opinion about what the project should look like but have to discuss it with group members before the final product is done. Explain that this is what happened with the Declaration: after the resolution to declare independence passed, the delegates went over the declaration itself word by word from July 2 until July 4, when they finally agreed on the final version and began signing it.

4. Work with students to read the **Declaration of Independence** (Handout 12B) and to complete **Analyzing Primary Sources** (Handout 12C). Help students to manage the length of the document by separating it into sections, focusing on the introductory section (already partially discussed in the previous lesson), the list of grievances, and the final Declaration in the last paragraph. Then use the following questions, based on the elements of reasoning, to discuss the document further:

♦ *How does the document introduce the purpose of the Declaration within the first few sentences? What words express the point of view of the Continental Congress?*

- *Which specific sentences in the introductory part of the document speak of the problem or issue?*

- *Why does Jefferson point out that "Prudence, indeed, will dictate that Governments long established should not be changed for light and transient causes"? How does this strengthen his argument?*

- *What are some of the specific pieces of evidence Jefferson provides in support of his argument?*

- *Does the evidence provided justify Jefferson's claim that King George III was a tyrant, unfit to be the ruler of a free people? Why or why not?*

- *Who was the intended audience? How do you know? How might different audiences have reacted to it?*

- *What consequences and implications might the document have had for its authors?*

5. Distribute copies of the **Standards of Reasoning** (Handout 12D; based on Paul, 1992). Explain to students that when we make an argument, it is not enough just to give reasons for our point of view; we need to make our reasons as strong and logical as we can. Have students work in groups to discuss the arguments presented in the Declaration according to the standards. (You may wish to have groups of students address different sections of the document OR have groups of students assess different standards and then share their ideas.)

Journal

Read the **July 3 Letter** (Handout 12E), an excerpt from a letter John Adams wrote to his wife Abigail, after the resolution to declare independence was passed. Then write a response to the following questions:

- *Which parts of John Adams' prediction in this letter came true? Which did not come true? Have you ever experienced an event that you knew would be remembered in history? What was the event, and why was it memorable?*

Homework

1. What are some of the predictable *effects* that would have been triggered by the Declaration of Independence? Once they had declared the United States to be an independent country,

what would Congress have to do next? Write a list of some major issues Congress would have to address.

2. Imagine you are a newspaper reporter in Philadelphia in July 1776. Write a front-page article describing the events and people's reactions. Use additional resources to help you find out more about reactions to the Declaration.

Extensions

1. Make a concept web for the concept of *liberty*.

2. Fifty-six men signed the Declaration of Independence. Choose several signers and find out about what happened to them afterward. What consequences did signing the Declaration have in their lives?

Assessment

♦ Primary source analysis
♦ Journal responses
♦ Participation in discussion

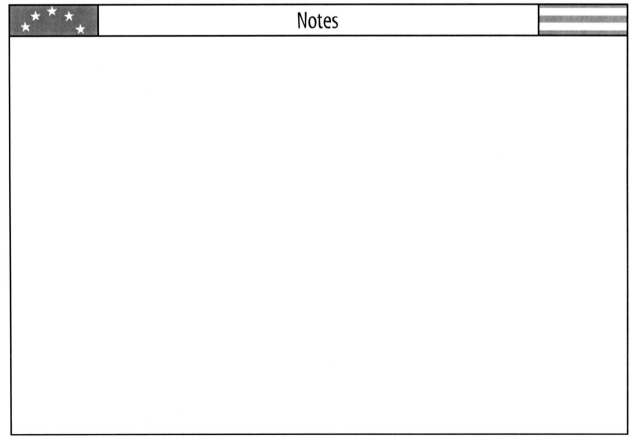

Notes

Resolutions from Virginia

That these United Colonies are, and of right ought to be, free and independent States, that they are absolved from all allegiance to the British Crown and that all political connection between them and the State of Great Britain is, and ought to be, totally dissolved.

That it is expedient forthwith to take the most effectual measures for forming foreign Alliances.

That a plan of confederation be prepared and transmitted to the respective Colonies for their consideration and approbation.

The Declaration of Independence

IN CONGRESS, JULY 4, 1776

The Unanimous Declaration of the Thirteen United States of America

WHEN IN THE COURSE OF HUMAN EVENTS, it becomes necessary for one people to dissolve the political bands which have connected them with another, and to assume among the powers of the earth, the separate and equal station to which the laws of Nature and of Nature's God entitle them, a decent respect to the opinions of mankind requires that they should declare the causes which impel them to the separation.

WE HOLD THESE TRUTHS TO BE SELF-EVIDENT, that all men are created equal, that they are endowed by their Creator with certain unalienable rights, that among these are life, liberty and the pursuit of happiness. That to secure these rights, governments are instituted among men, deriving their just powers from the consent of the governed, That whenever any form of government becomes destructive of these ends, it is the right of the people to alter or to abolish it, and to institute new government, laying its foundation on such principles and organizing its powers in such form, as to them shall seem most likely to effect their safety and happiness. Prudence, indeed, will dictate that governments long established should not be changed for light and transient causes; and accordingly all experience hath shown, that mankind are more disposed to suffer, while evils are sufferable, than to right themselves by abolishing the forms to which they are accustomed. But when a long train of abuses and usurpations, pursuing invariably the same object evinces a design to reduce them under absolute despotism, it is their right, it is their duty, to throw off such government, and to provide new guards for their future security.—Such has been the patient sufferance of these Colonies; and such is now the necessity which constrains them to alter their former systems of government. The history of the present King of Great Britain is a history of repeated injuries and usurpations, all having in direct object the establishment of an absolute tyranny over these States. To prove this, let facts be submitted to a candid world.

He has refused his assent to laws, the most wholesome and necessary for the public good.

He has forbidden his Governors to pass laws of immediate and pressing importance, unless suspended in their operation till his Assent should be obtained; and when so suspended, he has utterly neglected to attend to them.

He has refused to pass other Laws for the accommodation of large districts of people, unless those people would relinquish the right of representation in the legislature, a right inestimable to them and formidable to tyrants only.

He has called together legislative bodies at places unusual, uncomfortable, and distant from the depository of their public records, for the sole purpose of fatiguing them into compliance with his measures.

He has dissolved Representative Houses repeatedly, for opposing with manly firmness his invasions on the rights of the people.

He has refused for a long time, after such dissolutions, to cause others to be elected; whereby the legislative powers, incapable of annihilation, have returned to the people at large for their exercise; the State remaining in the mean time exposed to all the dangers of invasion from without, and convulsions within.

He has endeavored to prevent the population of these States; for that purpose obstructing the laws for naturalization of foreigners; refusing to pass others to encourage their migration hither, and raising the conditions of new appropriations of lands.

He has obstructed the administration of justice, by refusing his assent to laws for establishing judiciary powers.

He has made judges dependent on his will alone, for the tenure of their offices, and the amount and payment of their salaries.

He has erected a multitude of new offices, and sent hither swarms of officers to harass our people, and eat out their substance.

He has kept among us, in times of peace, standing armies without the Consent of our legislature.

He has affected to render the military independent of and superior to the civil power.

He has combined with others to subject us to a jurisdiction foreign to our constitution, and unacknowledged by our laws; giving his assent to their acts of pretended legislation:

For quartering large bodies of armed troops among us:

For protecting them, by a mock trial, from punishment for any Murders which they should commit on the inhabitants of these States:

For cutting off our trade with all parts of the world:

For imposing taxes on us without our consent:

For depriving us in many cases, of the benefits of trial by jury:

For transporting us beyond seas to be tried for pretended offenses:

For abolishing the free system of English laws in a neighboring province, establishing therein an arbitrary government, and enlarging its boundaries so as to render it at once an example and fit instrument for introducing the same absolute rule into these colonies:

For taking away our charters, abolishing our most valuable laws, and altering fundamentally the forms of our governments:

For suspending our own legislature, and declaring themselves invested with power to legislate for us in all cases whatsoever.

He has abdicated government here, by declaring us out of his protection and waging war against us.

He has plundered our seas, ravaged our coasts, burnt our towns, and destroyed the lives of our people.

He is at this time transporting large armies of foreign mercenaries to complete the works of death, desolation and tyranny, already begun with circumstances of cruelty and perfidy scarcely paralleled in the most barbarous ages, and totally unworthy the head of a civilized nation.

He has constrained our fellow citizens taken captive on the high seas to bear arms against their country, to become the executioners of their friends and brethren, or to fall themselves by their hands.

He has excited domestic insurrections amongst us, and has endeavored to bring on the inhabitants of our frontiers, the merciless Indian Savages, whose known rule of warfare, is an undistinguished destruction of all ages, sexes and conditions.

In every stage of these oppressions we have petitioned for redress in the most humble terms: Our repeated petitions have been answered only by repeated injury. A prince, whole character is thus marked by every act which may define a tyrant, is unfit to be the ruler of a free people.

Nor have we been wanting in attention to our British brethren. We have warned them from time to time of attempts by their legislature to extend an unwarrantable jurisdiction over us. We have reminded them of the circumstances of our emigration and settlement here. We have appealed to their native justice and magnanimity, and we have conjured them by the ties of our common kindred to disavow these usurpations, which, would inevitably interrupt our connections and correspondence. They too have been deaf to the voice of justice and of consanguinity. We must, therefore, acquiesce in the necessity, which denounces our separation, and hold them, as we hold the rest of mankind, enemies in war, in peace friends.

We, therefore, the Representatives of the United states of America, in General Congress, Assembled, appealing to the Supreme Judge of the world for the rectitude of our intentions, do, in the name, and by authority of the good people of these Colonies, solemnly publish and declare, That these United Colonies are, and of right ought to be Free and Independent States; that they are absolved from all allegiance to the British Crown, and that all political connection between them and the State of Great Britain, is and ought to be totally dissolved; and that as free and independent States, they have full power to levy war, conclude peace, contract alliances, establish commerce, and to do all other acts and things which independent States may of right do. And for the support of this Declaration, with a firm reliance on the protection of Divine Providence, we mutually pledge to each other our lives, our fortunes and our sacred honor.

Analyzing Primary Sources

Document Title:_____

Establishing a Context and Intent for the Source

Author:

Time (When was it written)?

Briefly describe the culture of the time and list related events of the time.

Purpose (Why was the document created?)

Audience (Who was the document created for?)

Understanding the Source

What problems/issues/events does the source address?

What are the main points/ideas/arguments?

What assumptions/values/feelings does the author reflect?

What actions/outcomes does the author expect? From whom?

Authenticity/Reliability (Could the source be invented, edited, or mistranslated? What corroborating evidence do you have about the source? Does the author know enough about the topic to discuss it?)

Representative (How typical is the source of others of the same period? What other information might you need to find this out?)

What could the consequences of this document be? (What would happen if the author's plans were carried out? What could happen to the author when people read this? How might this document affect or change public opinions?)

What were the actual consequences? What really happened as a result of this document?

 Short-term

 Long-term

What new or different interpretation does this source provide about the historical period?

Standards of Reasoning

- Are the reasons *clear*?

- Is the evidence *correct*?

- Are *specific* reasons or examples included rather than vague generalizations?

- Are the arguments and reasons *strong and important*?

- Is the thinking *logical*?

July 3 Letter

(From a letter from John Adams to Abigail Adams.)

Philadelphia, July 3, 1776

. . . The Second Day of July 1776, will be the most memorable Epocha, in the History of America. I am apt to believe that it will be celebrated, by succeeding generations, as the great anniversary Festival. It ought to be commemorated, as the Day of Deliverance by solemn Acts of devotion to God Almighty. It ought to be solemnized with Pomp and Parade, with Shows, Games, Sports, Guns, Bells, Bonfires and Illuminations from one End of this Continent to the other from this Time forward forever more.

You will think me transported with Enthusiasm but I am not. I am well aware of the Toil and Blood and Treasure, that it will cost us to maintain this Declaration, and support and defend these States. Yet through all the Gloom I can see the Rays of ravishing Light and Glory. I can see that the End is more than worth all the Means.

Source: Rhodehamel, *The American Revolution*, p. 127.

Stars, Stripes, and Rattlesnakes

Lesson 13

Curriculum Alignment

Goal 1	Goal 2	Goal 3	Goal 4	Goal 5
	X		X	X

Instructional Purpose

- ◆ To discuss implications of the Declaration of Independence
- ◆ To analyze the meaning of various symbols and flags used in the Revolution

Materials/Resources

1. Join or Die (Handout 13A)
2. Flag Features (Handout 13B)
3. Sample Flags (Handout 13C)
4. Internet Access

Vocabulary

flag—a piece of cloth of specific color and design, used as a symbol or emblem

symbol—something that represents another thing, especially a concrete object used to represent something abstract

union—(on a flag) a device or design, usually in the upper inner corner of a flag, representing the union or joining of two or more sovereign groups

Activities

1. Recall with students the section of the Virginia resolution from 1776 that recommended a plan of confederation to be drawn up for consideration by the various colonies. Emphasize to students that when the colonies declared themselves to be "free and independent states," there was no guarantee that those separate states would join together into one nation in the long run. (This may require some discussion of the term state and its meanings).

2. Share with students **Join or Die** (Handout 13A). Explain that this picture first appeared in the 1750s, as a comment on the Albany Plan of Union, in a newspaper published by Benjamin Franklin; the picture reappeared during the Revolutionary period. Have students work in groups to answer the questions on the page, and then discuss as a class, using the questions below:

    ◆ *What is a symbol? What are some important symbols you see every day? What are the purposes of those symbols?*

    ◆ *In what ways can a visual symbol be a stronger message than words?*

    ◆ *What is the main idea of the picture on the handout? How is the main idea communicated both in words and visually?*

    ◆ *Why do you think a rattlesnake was chosen as a symbol? In what ways could the colonies be compared to a rattlesnake?* (the view of the leaders promoting union was that separately the colonies could not rattle or be heard, but together they could be very powerful; also the idea that the colonies would not strike unless threatened)

3. Tell students that the rattlesnake became a popular symbol among the colonists in the period prior to and during the Revolution, and that many of the flags carried into battle by various groups of Revolutionary soldiers bore the rattlesnake symbol. Ask students to consider in what ways a flag serves as a symbol. Explain that during the Revolution, many different flags were used throughout the colonies and considered for the national flag. Tell students that in this lesson, they will explore some of these different flags and what was symbolized by their features.

4. Distribute copies of **Flag Features** (Handout 13B) and **Sample Flags** (Handout 13C). Divide students into groups, and explain that they should review the different flags and identify the key elements or symbols of them. They should complete the Flag Features handout by listing key elements of the different flags down the left-hand side, and the names of the flags on which each was found; they should then make inferences about the meaning of each element. Key elements should include both *pictures* and *phrases* (e.g., don't tread on me) as appropriate. (If possible, organize this activity with Internet access for all students—several web sites, listed at the end of the lesson, display many of the different Revolutionary flags in color with explanations.)

5. Share with students (orally or on an overhead) the following statement from the June 14, 1777 *Journal of Congress:* "Resolved that the flag of the U.S. be 13 stripes alternate red and white and the union be 13 stars in a blue field, representing a new constellation." Ask students the following questions:

   ♦ *Which flag does this resolution refer to? Did you explore that flag on your chart?* (Make sure students have an opportunity to view the flag referenced.)

   ♦ *What are the important symbolic pieces of this flag?*

6. For a math connection, ask students to think about how the early flag designers decided on the spatial layout of the flags. Have students explore the proportions of the original 13-star, 13-stripe flag. Visit the Betsy Ross website *(http://www.ushistory.org/betsy/index.html)* to explore with students how to cut out a perfect five-point star with just one snip of the scissors!

Journal

Which of the Revolutionary flags did you like best? Why? Why do you think the Congress adopted the flag it did?

Homework

1. A flag is one of many symbols a country might have for itself. Make a list of some American symbols (e.g., eagle, flag, Statue of Liberty, etc.) and write an explanation of why you think each is or is not a good symbol.

2. Be prepared to discuss details of the lives of soldiers as shown in your historical fiction reading in the next lesson.

Extensions

1. Find out about Betsy Ross, twice widowed in the Revolutionary War, who according to myth was the maker of the first American flag with the thirteen stripes and thirteen stars. Visit the Betsy Ross House website at *http://www.ushistory.org/betsy/index.html* and read the discussion of the myth of Betsy Ross.

2. Search newspaper archives and other news sources to find out about how and why a rattlesnake "Don't Tread on Me" flag has been used more recently by the American military.

3. Look at a collection of flags of the countries of the world, or of flags of the 50 states. What patterns do you see in the collections? What colors are most popular for flags? Which flags include a union in one corner? Is there a pattern to the ones that do?

Note to Teacher

The activity in this lesson for analyzing the features of different Revolutionary flags is most effectively done if students can have Internet access or access to resource books on Revolutionary flags. If such access is possible, the Sample Flags handout is not needed. Resources for exploring Revolutionary flags include the following websites:

http://www.walika.com/sr/flags/fedflags1.htm

http://americanrevolution.org/flags2.html

http://www.ushistory.org/betsy/flagpics.html

Another option is to have resource books available to students. Several are listed in the resources section at the end of the unit. In addition, there is a coloring book available of Revolutionary flags called *Flags to Color from the American Revolution* by Whitney Smith that may be of interest to students.

Assessment

- ◆ Flag chart
- ◆ Journal and homework responses

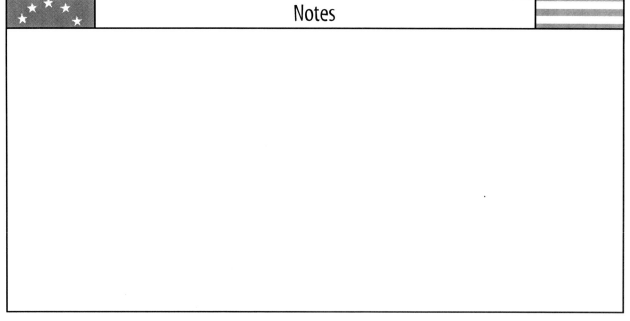
Notes

Join or Die

What do you see in the picture?	What does the picture *symbolize* or stand for?
What is the message of the picture?	**Why do you think the artist chose the *symbol* he did to communicate the message?**

Name_____ Date _____

Flag Features

13B

Feature or Element (may be a picture or words)	Names of Flags on Which It Appeared	Significance or Meaning

13C

Sample Flags

Bennington
1777

Culpeper
1775

Grand Union
1775

Gadsden
1776

Bunker Hill
1775

Source: *http://americanrevolution.org/flags2.html*

Soldiers' Lives in the Revolution

Curriculum Alignment

Goal 1	Goal 2	Goal 3	Goal 4	Goal 5
X	X	X	X	X

Instructional Purpose

- To discuss details of the lives of soldiers of the Revolution
- To compare fictional and nonfictional accounts of soldiers' lives
- To analyze the influence of military training on events of war

Materials/Resources

1. Hardships of War (Handout 14A)
2. Life as a Soldier (Handout 14B)
3. Student novels
4. Steuben's Drills (Handout 14C)

Vocabulary

drills—training of soldiers in tasks such as marching and using weapons

morale—the spirits of a person or group; the level of cheerfulness, confidence, and willingness to work

officer—a person in a position of authority or command in the armed forces

Activities

1. Remind students that while the Continental Congress was debating and declaring independence, the Continental Army continued to battle the British. Ask students to spend a few minutes writing down what they think life as a soldier in the Continental Army was like, based on what they know of the time period and what they have read in their historical fiction accounts.

2. Give students copies of **Hardships of War** (Handout 14A) and **Life as a Soldier** (Handout 14B). Have students work in groups to read the primary documents and to write details into the chart to describe each topic with relation to life in the army. Discuss responses, and then discuss the following questions:

   ◆ *What surprised you about the accounts from army life? What did not surprise you?*

   ◆ *How did the accounts compare to information you have learned about the lives of soldiers of the Revolution from your historical fiction readings?*

   ◆ *Why do you think the Continental Army was always so short of food?* (Share with students that throughout the war, there was difficulty in the supply chain, and Washington was always asking Congress to try to provide more supplies and appropriate pay for his men. Explain that one of Washington's greatest hardships in the war was keeping a large enough army, because soldiers would leave when their terms of enlistment were up or desert if conditions were too bad.)

   ◆ *How do you think the way the soldiers had to live affected the war? The outcomes of battles?*

   ◆ *How do you think life differed for the officers and the soldiers? How do you think life differed for the British troops and the American troops?*

   ◆ *How do you think the soldiers' lives were changed by their experiences?*

   ◆ *If you could talk to a soldier of the Continental Army, what would you ask him about?*

3. Point out to students that several of the sources they read related to the Army's experience at Valley Forge. Ask students what else they may know about this encampment, and explain that the Army camped at Valley Forge in the winter of 1777–1778 under very harsh conditions, and that many soldiers died. Yet historians agree that the months at Valley Forge were valuable and significant to the Continental Army despite the hardships, and the encampment has been referred to as the "Birthplace of an Army." Ask students what that description might mean, especially since the war had been going on for over two years by the time the army arrived at Valley Forge.

4. Explain to students that the officers in the army took advantage of the months at Valley Forge, when little fighting

occurred, to improve the army's training. Remind students that many of the soldiers came to the army as untrained volunteers, they were a mix of those who had militia experience and those who did not, and they were coming from thirteen different colonies with different perceptions of their unity. Tell students that although many of the leading officers in the army organized and supported the training, one of the most important influences on the army's improvement was Baron Friedrich von Steuben, a former Prussian army officer who had met with Benjamin Franklin in Paris and came to Valley Forge to work with the army in February 1778. Give students copies of **Steuben's Drills** (Handout 14C) and ask them to think about how each of Steuben's recommendations could strengthen an army's efficiency and effectiveness.

5. Discuss students' responses to the chart. Ask students to discuss the following:

   ◆ *What causes do you think affected the military leadership's decision to bring in foreign experts like von Steuben and to increase the army's training efforts?*

   ◆ *What do you think the effects of the increased training on the Continental soldiers would have been? What would have been the effects on their morale? What would have been the effects on their fighting skills? What about the effects on the overall war effort?*

6. Explain to students that the combination of stronger military training learned in the months at Valley Forge and the advantage the Americans had for frontier fighting instead of the traditional, field military style helped the Continental Army to hold out against the British, despite the British Army's larger numbers and more extensive training and supplies.

7. Provide time for students to work in their groups to complete their **Chronology of War** projects from Lesson 8. Students should present their projects at the beginning of the next lesson.

Journal

What decisions related to fighting in the war did characters in your novel have to make? Do you think the author of your book showed conditions for soldiers accurately, based on the primary sources you have read?

Homework

Imagine that you are a soldier of the Revolution camping at Valley Forge. Write a letter to someone at home talking about your experiences and your feelings.

Assessment

♦ Completed charts
♦ Journal and homework responses

Notes

Hardships of War

(From the march to Quebec, November 1775.)

Wednesday, Nov. 1st

Our greatest luxuries now consisted in a little water, stiffened with flour, in imitation of shoe-makers' paste, which was christened with the name of Lillipu. . . . We had now arrived as we thought to almost the zenith of distress. Several had been entirely destitute of either meat or bread for many days. . . .

Saturday, 4th

[We] visited an old peasant's house, where was a merry old woman at her loom, and two or three fine young girls. They were exceedingly rejoiced with our company. Bought some eggs, rum, sugar, sweetmeats, etc., where we made ourselves very happy. Upon the old woman being acquainted from whence we came, immediately fell singing and dancing "Yankee Doodle" with the greatest air of good humour. . . . We saluted her for her civilities, etc., marched.

—*Isaac Senter, surgeon, from Rhode Island*

(From the camp at New York, summer 1776.)

August 24. Before Noon I walked to the Place of Action, two Miles and a half. Like all earthly things, the Scenes of War are diverse and mixed. Some of our men were in Companies sitting under the shady Trees and conversing about the Occurrences of the Day: who were killed, or wounded, or taken Prisoners; and which Army, on the Whole, gained Ground or lost. Others were preparing their Victuals, and eating. Many were lying on the sides of the Hills opposite to the Enemy, and securely sleeping, while others, as it comes in turn, were standing among whistling Bullets, on the other Side of the Hills, taking Trees for their Security and shooting when they can.

—Philip Vickers Fithian, chaplain, New Jersey militia

(Journey to Valley Forge, December 1777.)

December 14. The Army which has been surprisingly healthy hitherto, now begins to grow sickly from the continued fatigues they have suffered this campaign. Yet they still show a spirit of Alacrity and Contentment not to be expected from so young Troops. I am Sick—discontented—and out of humour. Poor food—hard lodging—Cold Weather—fatigue—Nasty Clothes—nasty Cookery—vomit half my time. . . . I can't endure it—why are we sent here to starve and Freeze—What sweet Felicities have I left at home. A charming Wife—pretty Children—Good Beds—good food—good Cookery—all agreeable—all harmonious. Here all confusion—smoke and Cold—hunger and filthiness—a pox on my bad luck . . .

—Albigence Waldo, surgeon, Connecticut Continental regiment

(Arrival at Valley Forge, December 1777.)

We marched for the Valley Forge in order to take up our winter quarters. We were now in a truly forlorn condition—no clothing, no provisions, and as disheartened as need be. We arrived, however, at our destination a few days before Christmas. Our prospect was indeed dreary. In our miserable condition, to go into the wild woods and build us habitations to stay (not to live) in, in such a weak, starved, and naked condition, was appalling in the highest degree, especially to New Englanders, unaccustomed to such kind of hardships at home. . . .

We arrived at the Valley Forge in the evening; it was dark. There was no water to be found, and I was perishing with thirst. I searched for water till I was weary and came to my tent without finding any. Fatigue and thirst, joined with hunger, almost made me desperate. I felt at that instant as if I would have taken victuals or drink from the best friend I had on earth . . . At length I persuaded [two soldiers] to sell me a drink for three pence, Pennsylvania currency, which was every cent of property I could then call my own. . . .

—Joseph Plumb Martin, private, from Connecticut

(Letter from Washington at Valley Forge.)

To Governor George Clinton

Head Quarters, Valley Forge, February 16, 1778

Dear Sir: It is with great reluctance, I trouble you on a subject, which does not fall within your province; but it is a subject that occasions me more distress, than I have felt, since the commencement of the war; and which loudly demands the most zealous exertions of every person of weight and authority, who is interested in the success of our affairs. I mean the present dreadful situation of the army for want of provisions, and the miserable prospects before us, with respect to futurity. It is more alarming than you will probably conceive, for, to form a just idea, it were necessary to be on the spot. For some days past, there has been little less than a famine in camp. A part of the army has been a week, without any kind of flesh, and the rest for three or four days. Naked and starving as they are, we cannot enough admire the incomparable patience and fidelity of the soldiery, that they have not been ere this excited by their sufferings, to a general mutiny or dispersion. Strong symptoms, however, discontent have appeared in particular instances; and nothing but the most active efforts every where can long avert so shocking a catastrophe.

Sources: Rhodehamel, *The American Revolution*; Martin, *Private Yankee Doodle*; Monk, *Ordinary Americans*.

Life as a Soldier

Food and Drink	Clothing and Shelter
Activities	Emotions

Steuben's Drills

How would each part of Baron von Steuben's drills for the army help them to be more efficient and effective?

Drill	Influence
◆ Cut down the number of motions for reloading a musket from 19 to 15	
◆ Imposed standard pace for marching	
◆ Taught troops how to "wheel" in line to the right or left	
◆ Used a small model company for exhibition drills to the other soldiers	
◆ Emphasized officer responsibility for the well-being of their men	
◆ Emphasized care of weapons and equipment	

Alliance

 Lesson
15

Curriculum Alignment

Goal 1	Goal 2	Goal 3	Goal 4	Goal 5
X	X	X	X	X

Instructional Purpose

- ◆ To analyze the Continental Congress's desire to acquire support from foreign powers
- ◆ To explore different points of view on an alliance between the French and the Americans
- ◆ To trace major military events in the chronology of the war
- ◆ To develop skills in persuasive writing

Materials

1. Student projects on the Chronology of War
2. Reasoning about a Situation or Event (Handout 15A)
3. Celebrating the French Alliance (Handout 15B)

Vocabulary

diplomacy—the practice of conducting international relations, such as developing alliances and treaties among governments

Activities

1. Provide time for students to share their projects on the **Chronology of War** from Lesson 8. Encourage student groups to set up their posters and allow group members to spend some time presenting and some time rotating to hear presentations from other groups. Add major events from the presentations to the unit timeline, and ask students if they can make generalizations about the progress of the war based on what they studied. Ask questions such as the following: *Which side seemed to win more actual battles? How did the differences in fighting style affect the outcome of battles? What advantages did the Americans have? What advantages did the British have?*

2. Ask students to use what they have learned so far in the unit and their own prior knowledge to make a list of some of the *needs of war*—the things a government needs in order to wage a successful war against another government. Brainstorm a list on the board with students. Discuss the following questions as needed to expand on the ideas students generated:

   ♦ *What are the needs of war in terms of **human resources**?*

   ♦ *What are the needs of war in terms of **natural resources**?*

   ♦ *What are the needs of war in terms of **capital or financial resources**?*

   ♦ *In what ways are the needs of war different based on the geographical area of the fighting?*

3. Have students think about where Congress could get access to all these needed resources during the Revolution. Explain that the new United States was limited in terms of *population* supporting the war and in terms of *financial resources*. In addition, the U.S. had only a very limited navy, while the British Navy ruled oceans around the world. Ask students to think about the implications of these areas of need and how the Congress might have been able to find ways to meet these needs.

4. Ask students what the word *diplomacy* means. Explain that in discussing governments, diplomacy refers to the discussions and agreements that representatives of governments work to make with one another, for the benefit of both or all countries involved. Tell students that during the Revolution, the Continental Congress sent diplomats to other countries to try to work out treaties that would help the Americans to wage their revolution successfully. Explain that diplomats were sent to several different governments of Europe, primarily those countries that were Britain's greatest enemies *(Why?)*, and most importantly the government of France.

5. Distribute copies of **Reasoning about a Situation or Event** (Handout 15A). Ask students to use this chart to think about the issue France was faced with during the Revolution: should France openly support the American Revolution through publicly acknowledging the United States and through providing military and financial support? Work with students to identify key stakeholders (e.g., Congress, France, Britain) and to detail their likely perspectives on this issue. Make sure to discuss with students that France and Britain

were enemies, but that in some ways it was dangerous for the French king to support a revolution *against* a king.

6. Tell students that the French supported the Americans quietly for much of the war, especially after Benjamin Franklin went to Paris in 1776 to support American interests, but that the French government did not publicly declare their support and enter an alliance until early 1778. Discuss with students the following:

   ◆ *Why do you think the French waited so long to enter a formal alliance with the Americans?*

   ◆ *In what ways could the Declaration of Independence have helped to promote the French alliance?* (work with students to understand the different implications of supporting a rebellion and supporting a war between two nations, even if one of the nations was not yet widely recognized)

   ◆ *In what ways could American military actions have influenced the French alliance?*

   ◆ *What would be the benefits to the French of entering an alliance with the United States?*

7. Have students pretend that they are committees within Congress writing a letter to the French king to ask his support of the Revolutionary cause. Determine a specific time during the war that the letter is to be written, and encourage students to use their timelines to confirm what events had already happened by the time of their letter-writing. (You may wish to have different groups of students write with different assigned dates.) Tell students to organize their letters using the Hamburger Model, preparing the letters to include an introduction, at least three reasons with elaboration, and a conclusion. Encourage them to take on the role of the Congressional members, recognizing that they do not know the outcome of the war yet and that they are writing to a *king*.

8. Ask students to share their letters. Then tell students that the American victory at Saratoga was one of the most important influences on the French, demonstrating the commitment of the American army and its potential to win against the British. In early 1778, the French entered a formal alliance with the Americans, supplying troops, ships, and supplies to support the Continental Army for the remainder of the war.

9. Give students copies of **Celebrating the French Alliance** (Handout 15B) and have students read. Then ask students the following questions:

   ◆ *What does this letter show about the army's reaction to the alliance with the French? Why was the alliance with the French such a cause for celebration?*

   ◆ *What else does this letter reveal about the lives of soldiers in the army?* (Encourage students to add any extra details to their charts from the previous lesson.) *What does it show about the training of the troops?*

Homework

Imagine again (as in Lesson 11) that you are a newspaper reporter in Philadelphia. Write a report of the news of the French alliance and people's reaction to it.

Extension

Find out about Benjamin Franklin's time in France and how he promoted different images of Americans to help strengthen his cause.

Notes to Teacher

1. Students may require some additional background reading on the diplomatic situation in order to complete the reasoning chart about the issues. A summary of the French-American alliance issue in an American history textbook should be sufficient to support sufficient understanding to complete the chart.

2. This lesson will take more than one class period with the project presentations.

Assessment

   ◆ Group project completion and presentation
   ◆ Reasoning chart
   ◆ Persuasive letter

Notes

Name_____ Date _____

H a n d o u t

Reasoning about a Situation or Event

15A

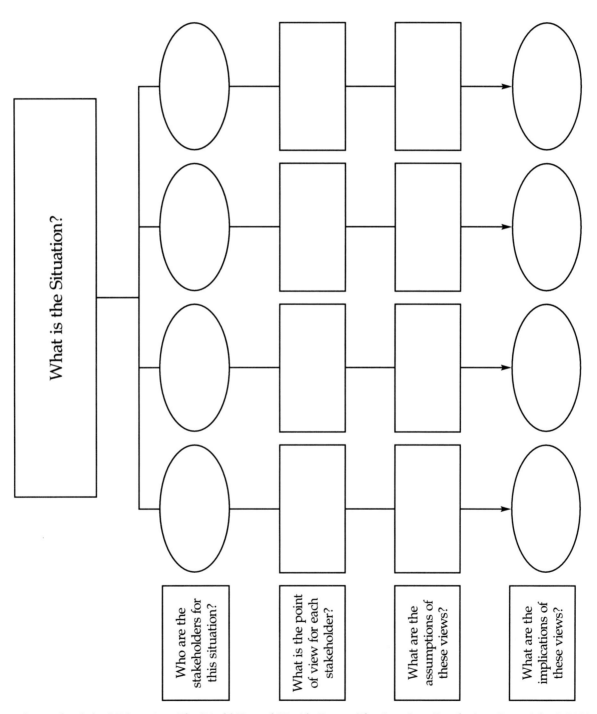

What is the Situation?

Who are the stakeholders for this situation?

What is the point of view for each stakeholder?

What are the assumptions of these views?

What are the implications of these views?

From Center for Gifted Education, *The World Turned Upside Down: The American Revolution.* Copyright © 2003 Kendall/Hunt Publishing Company—may be reproduced by individual teachers for classroom use only.

221

Name_____ Date _____ H a n d o u t

Celebrating the French Alliance

15B

(From a letter from John Laurens, aide to General Washington, to his father.)

Valley Forge, May 7, 1778

My dear Father.

Yesterday we celebrated the new alliance with as much splendor as the short notice would allow. Divine service preceded the rejoicing. After a proper pause, the several brigades marched by their right to the posts in order of battle—and the line was formed with admirable rapidity and precision—three Salutes of Artillery, thirteen each, and three general discharges of a running fire by the musketry, were given in honor of the King of France—the friendly European powers—and the United American States—loud huzzas.

The order with which the whole was conducted—the beautiful effect of the running fire which was executed to perfection—the martial appearance of the Troops—gave sensible pleasure to every one present—the whole was managed by signal, and the plan as formed by Baron de Steuben succeeded in every particular, which is in a great measure to be attributed to his unwearied attention and to the visible progress which the troops have already made under his discipline.

A cold collation was given afterwards at which all the officers of the Army and some Ladies of the neighborhood were present—Triumph beamed in every countenance—the greatness of mind and policy of Louis XVI were extol'd—and his long life toasted with as much sincerity as that of the British King used to be in former times. The General received such proofs of the love and attachment of his officers as must have given him the most exquisite feelings. . . .

Source: Rhodehamel, *The American Revolution,* p. 414.

Women at Home and at the Front

Curriculum Alignment

Goal 1	Goal 2	Goal 3	Goal 4	Goal 5
X	X	X	X	X

Instructional Purpose

- ◆ To explore the experiences of women of the Revolutionary period
- ◆ To analyze the influences of family on the actions of soldiers and officers of the war
- ◆ To discuss the continuance of daily life despite war and global change

Materials

1. Johnny Has Gone for a Soldier (Handout 16A)
2. Analyzing Primary Sources (Handout 16B)
3. Patriot Women of the Revolution (Handout 16C–16H)
4. Women's Lives (Handout 16I)

Vocabulary

camp follower—a civilian who follows a unit of the military from place to place

homefront—the context and activities of civilians in a country at war

Activities

1. Ask students what they think life was like for women during the Revolutionary War.

   - ◆ *What do you know about the roles women played during the Revolution?*
   - ◆ *What information or evidence do you already have about women's lives?*
   - ◆ *What additional assumptions would you make about their lives?*

   Have students read the words (and listen to a recording, if possible) of the song **"Johnny Has Gone for a Soldier"** (Handout 16A). Ask students the following questions:

   - ◆ *What feelings does this song demonstrate?*

- *What actions does the song suggest the speaker will take? What is she trying to do for Johnny? Why?*

- *In what ways do you think women of the Revolutionary period were able to help their loved ones who went to be soldiers? How would their lives change when their loved ones went away?*

- *How would the implications of war have been different for men and for women during the Revolution? How were they similar?*

2. Divide students into groups and give each group **Analyzing Primary Sources** (Handout 16B) and at least two different documents from among the **Patriot Women of the Revolution** documents (Handouts 16C, 16D, 16E, 16F, 16G, 16H). Explain that some of these documents were written *by* women during the period, while others were written *about* women (students should check the source information). Once they have analyzed their documents, student groups should prepare brief summaries of their discussions to share with students from other groups.

3. Reorganize students into groups again, so that each group includes a student who read each of the different documents. Have students share the summaries of their group work, then have them work with the new groups to determine major *effects* of the Revolution on women's lives and possible causes of those effects for the **Women's Lives** chart (Handout 16I).

4. Debrief the activity with students, using questions such as the following:

- *What generalizations, if any, can you make about the lives of Patriot women during the Revolution and the effects of the major events on their lives? On what evidence do you base your conclusions?*

- *In what ways were the hardships faced by women similar to the hardships faced by men at the front? In what ways were they different?*

- *How do you think the lives of soldiers and the delegates to Congress were affected by their thoughts of their families at home?*

- *What new roles or responsibilities did women have to take on because of the events of the Revolution?*

- *How do you think the Revolution would have been affected if women such as those you read about did not support the war? Why?*

- *How was the information you read about women in these documents similar to or different from information you have learned from reading your historical fiction selections? What influences might have affected those similarities and differences?*

5. Have students recall the activity they did for homework in Lesson 14 in which they pretended to be soldiers at Valley Forge and wrote letters home. Have them exchange those letters so that each student has a different student's letter. Ask them to read their letter and then write a response to it, taking on the role of a woman at home during the war. Encourage them to identify the place they are living and base some of the content of their letter on experiences they might have had in that area. Ask students to finish their letters for homework and "send them back" in the next class.

Journal

Think about ways women can be involved in the military and with military operations today. Discuss some ways that their opportunities and experiences are *similar* to as well as *different from* the experiences of women in the Revolutionary period.

Homework

1. Finish your letter from the "home front."

2. Finish your historical fiction assignment for sharing in the next lesson.

Extension

The documents from this lesson were all focused on Patriot women. Find out about the lives of some Loyalist women during the war and compare their experiences to the ones you read about for the Patriot women.

Note to Teacher

The documents in this lesson vary in difficulty and length; you may choose to assign them to student groups based on difficulty, but ensure that each group gets a diverse picture of women's experiences.

Assessment

◆ Primary source analysis and summary chart
◆ Participation in discussion
◆ Letters

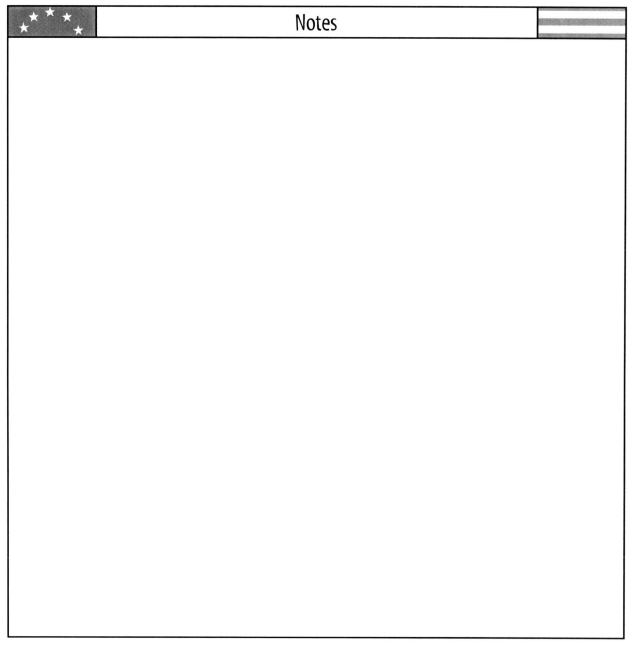

Notes

Johnny has Gone for a Soldier

(From an Irish folk song, popular with soldiers in the American Revolution and in the Civil War.)

Here I sit on Buttermilk Hill
Who can blame me, cryin' my fill
And ev'ry tear would turn a mill,
Johnny has gone for a soldier.

Me, oh my, I loved him so,
Broke my heart to see him go,
And only time will heal my woe,
Johnny has gone for a soldier.

I'll sell my rod, I'll sell my reel,
Likewise I'll sell my spinning wheel,
And buy my love a sword of steel,
Johnny has gone for a soldier.

I'll dye my dress, I'll dye it red,
And through the streets I'll beg for bread,
For the lad that I love from me has fled,
Johnny has gone for a soldier.

Source: *http://www.contemplator.com/folk/johnny.html.*

Analyzing Primary Sources

Document Title:_____

Establishing a Context and Intent for the Source

> Author:
>
> Time (When was it written)?
>
> Briefly describe the culture of the time and list related events of the time.
>
> Purpose (Why was the document created?)
>
> Audience (Who was the document created for?)

Understanding the Source

> What problems/issues/events does the source address?
>
> What are the main points/ideas/arguments?
>
> What assumptions/values/feelings does the author reflect?
>
> What actions/outcomes does the author expect? From whom?

Authenticity/Reliability (Could the source be invented, edited, or mistranslated? What corroborating evidence do you have about the source? Does the author know enough about the topic to discuss it?)

Representative (How typical is the source of others of the same period? What other information might you need to find this out?)

What could the consequences of this document be? (What would happen if the author's plans were carried out? What could happen to the author when people read this? How might this document affect or change public opinions?)

What were the actual consequences? What really happened as a result of this document?

Short-term

Long-term

What new or different interpretation does this source provide about the historical period?

Patriot Women of the Revolution: Sarah Osborn

(Sarah Osborn was a "camp-follower," or a woman who traveled with the Continental Army, helping the soldiers by cooking, cleaning, and so forth. This is her account of events at the time of the siege of Yorktown.)

We marched immediately for a place called Williamsburg, . . . myself alternately on horseback and on foot. There arrived, we remained two days till the army all came in by land and then marched for Yorktown. . . . The New York troops were posted at the right, the Connecticut troops next, and the French to the left. In about one day or less than a day, we reached the place of encampment about one mile from Yorktown. . . . I took my stand just back of the American tents, say about a mile from the town, and busied myself washing, mending, and cooking for the soldiers, in which I was assisted by other females. Some men washed their own clothing. I heard the roar of the artillery for a number of days, and the last night the Americans threw up entrenchments; it was a misty, foggy night, rather wet but not rainy. . . . I cooked and carried in beef, bread, and coffee (in a gallon pot) to the soldiers in the entrenchment.

On one occasion when I was thus employed carrying in provisions, I met General Washington, who asked me if I "was not afraid of the cannonballs?"

I replied, . . . "It would not do for the men to fight and starve too."

Source: Monk, *Ordinary Americans,* p. 37.

Patriot Women of the Revolution: Distress of Families

(Excerpt from letter from General Nathaniel Greene to his wife Catherine, written in South Carolina, January 1781.)

You can have no idea of the distress and misery that prevails in this quarter. Hundreds of families that formerly lived in great opulence and now reduced to beggary and want. A Gentleman from Georgia was this morning with me, to get assistance to move his wife and family out of the Enemy's way. They have been separated for upwards of eight months, during all which time the wife never heard from her husband, nor the husband from his wife. Her distress was so great that she has been obliged to sell all her plate, table linen, and even wearing apparel, to maintain her poor little children. In this situation she was tantalised by the Tories, and insulted by the British. . . .

Source: Rhodehamel, *The American Revolution,* p. 654.

Patriot Women of the Revolution: Near the Battle

(From the journal of Sarah Wister, who lived near Philadelphia and with her family hosted and fed some of the Continental Army officers as they traveled through the area.)

December 5, 1777

Oh gracious I am all alive with fear. The English have come out to attack (as we imagine) our army. They are on Chestnut Hill our army three mile this side, what will become of us. Only six mile distant, we are in hourly expectation of an engagement. I fear we shall be in the midst of it—heaven defend us from so dreadful a sight. The battle of Germantown and the horrors of that day are recent in my mind. It will be sufficiently dreadful if we are only in hearing of the firing to think how many of our fellow creatures are plung'd into the boundless ocean of eternity, few of them prepar'd to meet their fate but they are summon'd before an all merciful judge from whom they have a great deal to hope.

Source: Rhodehamel, *The American Revolution,* p. 391.

Patriot Women of the Revolution: Molly Pitcher

(From the memoirs of Joseph Plumb Martin, Connecticut soldier, summer 1778; describing the actions of Mary Ludwig Hayes, who also carried water for soldiers, earning the nickname Molly Pitcher.)

One little incident happened during the heat of the cannonade, which I was eyewitness to, and which I think would be unpardonable not to mention. A woman whose husband belonged to the artillery and who was then attached to a piece in the engagement, attended with her husband at the piece the whole time. While in the act of reaching a cartridge and having one of her feet as far before the other as she could step, a cannon shot from the enemy passed directly between her legs without doing any other damage than carrying away all the lower part of her petticoat. Looking at it with apparent unconcern, she observed that it was lucky it did not pass a little higher, for in that case it might have carried away something else, and continued her occupation.

Source: Martin, *Private Yankee Doodle,* p. 132.

Patriot Women of the Revolution: Deborah Sampson

16G

(From a New York newspaper, January 10, 1784.)

An extraordinary instance of virtue in a female soldier has occurred lately in the American army, in the Massachusetts line . . . a lively, comely young nymph, 19 years of age, dressed in man's apparel, has been discovered, and what redounds to her honor, she has served in the character of a soldier for nearly three years undiscovered. During this time, she displayed much alertness, chastity, and valor: having been in several engagements and received two wounds, a small shot remaining in her to this day. She was a remarkable, vigilant soldier on her post, always gained the applause of her officers, was never found in liquor, and always kept company with the most temperate and upright soldiers. For several months, this gallantress served with credit in a general officer's family. A violent illness, when the troops were at Philadelphia, led to the discovery of her sex. She has since been honorably discharged from the army, with a reward, and sent to her connections, who, it appears, live to the eastward of Boston at a place called Meduncock.

The cause of her impersonating a man, it is said, proceeded from the rigor of her parents, who exerted their prerogative to induce her marriage with a young gentleman against whom she had conceived a great antipathy, together with her being a remarkable heroine and warmly attached to the cause of her country; in the service of which it must be acknowledged, she gained reputation, and, no doubt, will be noticed in the history of our grand revolution. . . .

Source: Monk, *Ordinary Americans,* p. 35.

Name_____ Date _____

Patriot Women of the Revolution: Abigail Adams

(From a letter from Abigail Adams in Massachusetts to John Adams in Congress in Philadelphia, March 31, 1776.)

. . . I long to hear that you have declared an independency—and by the way in the new Code of Laws which I suppose it will be necessary for you to make I desire you would Remember the Ladies, and be more generous and favorable to them than your ancestors. Do not put such unlimited power in the hands of the Husbands. Remember all Men would be tyrants if they could. If particular care and attention is not paid to the Ladies we are determined to foment a Rebellion, and will not hold ourselves bound by any Laws in which we have no voice, or Representation.

That your Sex are Naturally Tyrannical is a Truth so thoroughly established as to admit of no dispute, but such of you as wish to be happy willingly give up the harsh title of Master for the more tender and endearing one of Friend. Why then, not put it out of the power of the vicious and the Lawless to use us with cruelty and indignity with impunity. Men of Sense in all Ages abhor those customs which treat us only as the vassals of your Sex. Regard us then as Beings placed by providence under your protection and in imitation of the Supreme Being make use of that power only for our happiness.

Source: Rhodehamel, *The American Revolution*, pp. 117–118.

Women's Lives

Effects of the Revolution on Women's Lives	Potential *Causes* of these Effects	Possible Long-Term Implications

A Civil War? Patriots and Tories

Curriculum Alignment

Goal 1	Goal 2	Goal 3	Goal 4	Goal 5
X	X	X	X	X

Instructional Purpose

- ♦ To understand the different perspectives of Patriots and Tories on events and circumstances of the Revolution
- ♦ To use persuasive writing to express a point of view on Revolutionary issues

Materials

1. Reasoning Web (Handout 17A)
2. The Rebels (Handout 17B)
3. Banishing Tories (Handout 17C)
4. Patriots and Loyalists (Handout 17D)

Vocabulary

Loyalist—an American colonist who favored the British side during the Revolution; also called Tory

Rebel—a person involved in a rebellion or resistance against an established government; term used by the British to refer to the Patriots during the Revolution

Tory—an American colonist loyal to the British cause during the Revolution; also called Loyalist

Activities

1. Give students opportunities to share their historical fiction assignments, having them meet in small groups or with the whole group to share their persuasive essays about whether or not they would recommend their books to others.

2. Have students get into groups with other students who read the same historical fiction selections. Ask students to discuss in their groups what their books revealed about Patriots and Tories and their different views of the war and one another. Invite the different groups to share important details from their discussions.

3. Tell students that the American Revolution was not a popular cause among all of the American colonists. Historians estimate that around one third of Americans were Tories, or Loyalists, who were loyal to the British; one third were Patriots, supporting the American cause; and another third did not visibly support either side. Use elements on the **Reasoning Web** (Handout 17A) and the following questions to guide discussion:

   ◆ *Do you think the decision to support or not to support the Revolution would have been a difficult one? Why or why not?*

   ◆ *Why do you think there was so much division among the Americans?*

   ◆ *What were potential implications of supporting the war? What were potential implications of not supporting the war?*

   ◆ *What were the implications of so many Americans loyal to the British during the war? How would that affect the way the war was conducted? How would it affect the actual fighting? How would it affect supply chains and information networks?*

4. Ask students to think of examples of times when there has been disagreement within the school or community on an important issue. *What was the issue? What were some of the feelings involved? Did different sides make fun of one another and/or share harsh criticism in the press?* Distribute copies of **The Rebels** (Handout 17B) and **Banishing Tories** (Handout 17C). Explain that these documents both show how strong the feelings of the two groups became against one another. Have students work in groups to read the documents and complete **Patriots and Loyalists** (Handout 17D).

5. Explain to students that they are now to write two short accounts of one major event during the war, writing one account from a Patriot perspective and one account from a Loyalist perspective. They may choose a major event that they have studied in class or through their project (e.g., the start of the war, the signing of the Declaration, one of the bat-

tles, the French alliance, etc.), and they can choose for their accounts to write diary entries, letters, newspaper accounts, or some other format, but their content should reflect their format. Encourage students to begin drafting their accounts and to finish them for homework.

Journal

Did reading your historical fiction piece change your thinking about the Revolution in any way? How? What impression did you get from your book about "good guys" and "bad guys"?

Homework

Finish writing your accounts from the Patriot and the Loyalist point of view.

Extension

Because Americans had differing of points of view about the war, it was very difficult to know who to trust. Beyond anger within communities between neighbors with different points of view, there were spies for both sides who watched for information they could share with their leaders to give their side an advantage. Find out about some of the spies of the Revolution, what they did, and what happened to them.

Assessment

♦ Reasoning web
♦ Chart
♦ Written accounts of events

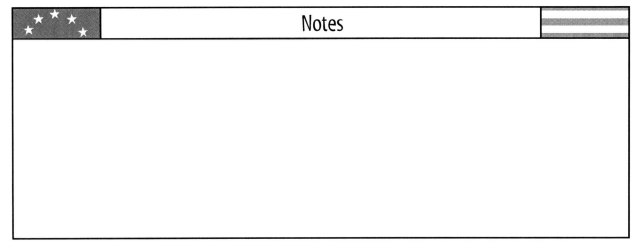

Notes

Reasoning Web

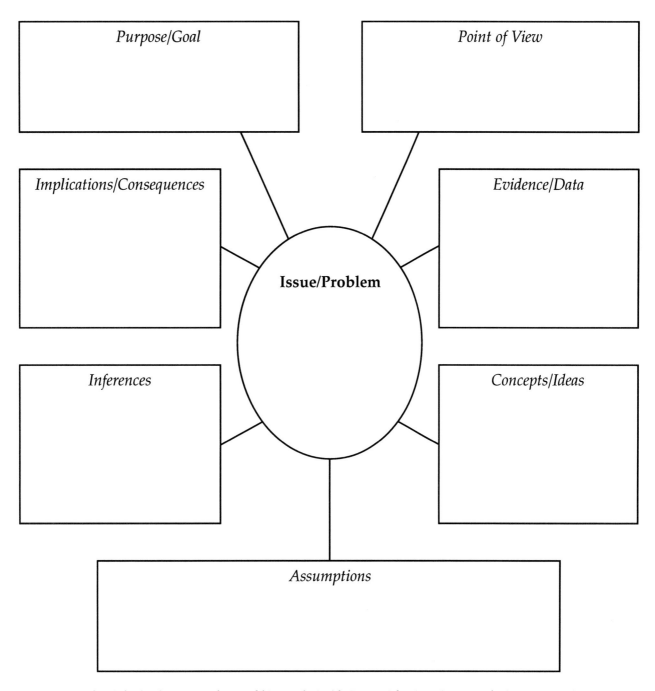

The Rebels

(From a song written by Captain Smyth of a branch of Loyalist troops in 1778.)

Ye brave, honest subjects, who dare to be loyal

And have stood the brunt of every trial

Of hunting-shirts and rifle guns:

Come listen awhile, and I'll sing you a song;

I'll show you those Yankees are all in the wrong,

Who, with blustering look and most awkward gait,

'Gainst their lawful sovereign dare for to prate,

With their hunting-shirts and rifle-guns. . . .

For one lawful ruler, many tyrants we've got,

Who force young and old to their wars, to be shot,

With their hunting-shirts and rifle-guns.

Our good king, God speed him! Never used men so;

We then could speak, act, and like freemen could go;

But committees enslave us, our Liberty's gone,

Our trade and church murdered, our country's undone,

With their hunting-shirts and rifle-guns. . . .

Source: Bruun and Crosby, *Our Nation's Archive,* pp. 137–138.

Banishing Tories

(From a letter appearing in the newspaper *The Pennsylvania Packet,* August 5, 1779.)

. . . I can no longer be silent on this subject, and see the independence of my country, after standing every shock from without, endangered by internal enemies. Rouse, America! your danger is great—great from a quarter where you least expect it. The Tories—the Tories will yet be the ruin of you. 'Tis high time they were separated from among you. They are now busily engaged in undermining your liberties. They have a thousand ways of doing it, and they make use of them all. Who were the occasion of this war? the Tories. Who persuaded the tyrant of Britain to prosecute it in a manner before unknown to civilized nations and shocking even to barbarians? the Tories. . . . Who have always counteracted the endeavours of Congress to secure the liberty of this country? the Tories. . . . Awake, Americans, to a sense of your danger. No time is to be lost— Instantly banish every Tory from among you. . . . Send them where they may enjoy their beloved slavery in perfection. Send them to the island of Britain, there let them drink the cup of slavery and eat the bread of bitterness all the days of their existence. . . . Never let them taste the sweets of that independence which they strove to prevent. . . .

Source: Rhodehamel, *The American Revolution,* pp. 530–532.

Patriots and Loyalists

	The Rebels	Banishing Tories
What impressions does the document give of the group it *criticizes*?		
What impressions does the document give of the side it *represents*?		
What point of view does the document show about the concept of *freedom*?		
What point of view does the document show about *leadership and government* for the colonies?		
What *emotions* does the document play on to try to convince people of a certain point of view? (for example, how does it use *pride* or *fear* or some other emotion?		

Liberty for All?

 Lesson 18

Curriculum Alignment

Goal 1	Goal 2	Goal 3	Goal 4	Goal 5
	X		X	X

Instructional Purpose

- ◆ To identify and analyze implications of Revolutionary events for African Americans
- ◆ To discuss Native American decisions around the Revolutionary War

Materials

1. Reasoning about a Situation or Event (Handout 18A)
2. Stockbridge Speech (Handout 18B)
3. Poem to George Washington (Handout 18C)
4. Washington's Reply (Handout 18D)

Vocabulary

present-mindedness—the application of current values and ideals to events and contexts of the past, without consideration of the values and ideals influencing those events at the time of their occurrence

Activities

1. Recall students' attention to the statement in the Declaration of Independence that asserted that "all men are created equal." Ask students if they can identify any ways in which we might today perceive some contradiction in that statement. Remind students that at the time of the Revolution, many wealthier Americans owned slaves, including some of the signers of the Declaration of Independence and including the Northern as well as the Southern states.

2. Emphasize to students that when we study history, it is important for us to recognize that some of our present values and ideals are different from the values and ideals of the people we are studying. Although we may disagree with the values and ideals of the past, we

need to try to understand them in order to fully understand the events and their implications. At the time of the Revolution, only a small number of Americans had begun to question the idea of slavery, and although the American colonists had developed some cordial relations (and some less cordial) with the Native Americans, the colonists of European descent still did not see these groups as equal or really closely linked in the same cause.

3. Explain to students that during the Revolutionary War, the British and Continental Armies both considered ways to use the African American population to their advantage. Both sides advertised opportunities for slaves to earn their freedom by fighting in the war, and both sides faced opposition from Southern landowners for the idea of arming the black population. Divide the class into two groups. Give each group a copy of **Reasoning about a Situation or Event** (Handout 18A). Assign one group the situation that early in the war, several British leaders, most prominently the royal governor of Virginia Lord Dunmore, offered freedom to slaves who deserted their masters and volunteered to fight for Britain. Assign the other group the situation that the Continental Congress voted in 1779 to raise regiments of black soldiers in Georgia and South Carolina by offering them their freedom after service in the war. Provide students with reference materials as needed, to help them think through the points of view and implications of key stakeholders within these situations.

4. Discuss students' completed charts. Use questions such as the following to help guide the discussion.

   ♦ *How would Southern landowners have responded to these two plans? Why?*

   ♦ *Why was it important for Congress and for the British to keep Southern landowners who supported them happy?*

   ♦ *How do you think African Americans would have responded to the language of the Declaration of Independence?*

   ♦ *At the time of the Revolution, the British also ruled the West Indies, where slavery was even more brutal than in the American South. How do you think this information would have influenced the point of view of African Americans on their options?*

   ♦ *Before the end of the war, some Northern states had already passed laws abolishing slavery and others were beginning to move plans forward to abolish it. How do you think the events of the Revolution and the participation of African Americans in the war might have affected these decisions?*

5. Tell students that another important influence on events and decisions of the Revolutionary period was the perspective of the various Native American groups living in the regions of the colonies. The colonists and the British had had to establish relationships with the Native Americans throughout the colonial period; some of these relationships were positive and others were more strained. Have students read the **Stockbridge Speech** (Handout 18B), given to the Massachusetts Congress in 1775 by a member of the Stockbridge tribe. Ask students to consider the following questions:

   ◆ *What does this document show about the relationship between the Stockbridge Indians and the colonists?*

   ◆ *What does the speaker mean about "fighting his own way"? How was the Native American way of fighting different from the British and the American militia?*

   ◆ *What might have been some reasons for Native Americans to support the colonists in the war? What might have been some reasons for them to support the British?*

   ◆ *What were some potential implications for the Native Americans of the eastern part of North America if the British won the war? if the Americans won the war? How might their lives change, either way?*

6. In preparation for the "Gallery of Greats" sharing in the next lesson, tell students that on their list of famous people from the Revolution, there were some who interacted regularly, some who never met each other, and some who interacted in more unusual ways. Tell students that Phyllis Wheatley was an important figure of the Revolutionary period in several ways; not only was she an important Patriot poet, she was also the first African American writer to be published. Share with students the excerpt from **Wheatley's Poem to George Washington** (Handout 18C) and **Washington's Reply** (Handout 18D). Then have students work in groups to answer the following questions:

   ◆ *What can you tell about these two individuals from these written documents?*

   ◆ *What impressions do they give of each person?*

- *If you did not know anything about George Washington and the first thing you read was Phyllis Wheatley's poem, what would you think about him?*

- *What does that tell you about the importance of considering point of view and bias when you are reading documents?*

7. Share with students more about the background of Phyllis Wheatley (see *http://www.jmu.edu/madison/wheatley/* for more information). Then invite students to write poems about Wheatley herself.

Journal

Historians talk about the importance of avoiding *present-mindedness* in studying history. What are some of the ways in which we have to be careful about present-mindedness when we are studying the Revolutionary period? In other words, what are some of the actions and events that are very hard to understand or accept if we look at them with 21st-century eyes?

Homework

Finish your biography project for sharing in the next class.

Extensions

1. Learn more about the contributions of African Americans and Native Americans to the Revolutionary War events. How did their participation influence outcomes for both sides?

2. Find out more about how "frontier warfare" influenced the outcomes of the war. How did their history of interaction with Native Americans help the Continentals to succeed in battle against the British?

3. Research statistics on African American participation in American wars. Find out approximately what percentage of the fighting force in each major war has been African American, and also what percentage of the total population African Americans were at each time period. Write a summary that traces how opportunities for military participation have changed for African Americans over the course of American history.

Notes to Teacher

1. If a student chose Phyllis Wheatley as the subject for a biography project, the last part of this lesson should be modified appropriately to allow the student to share the project. In sharing the poem with students, based on student facility with the language, you may wish to share only the last stanza to minimize time spent comprehending the piece and enhance time spent discussing the inferences to be drawn from it.

2. The concept of present-mindedness in studying history is complex, but it is important for students to begin to consider how the writers of the Declaration of Independence were at once men of their time and ahead of their time. You may wish to share with students that an 1862 history of African American participation in the Revolution reportedly helped to influence Lincoln in issuing the Emancipation Proclamation.

Assessment

*   Reasoning chart
*   Poem
*   Participation in discussion
*   Journal response

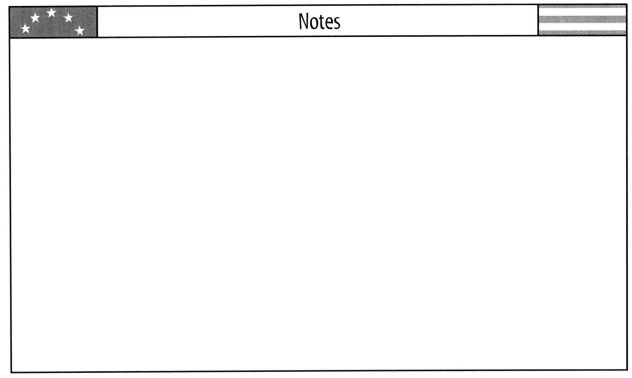

Notes

Name_____ Date _____   H a n d o u t

Reasoning about a Situation or Event

18A

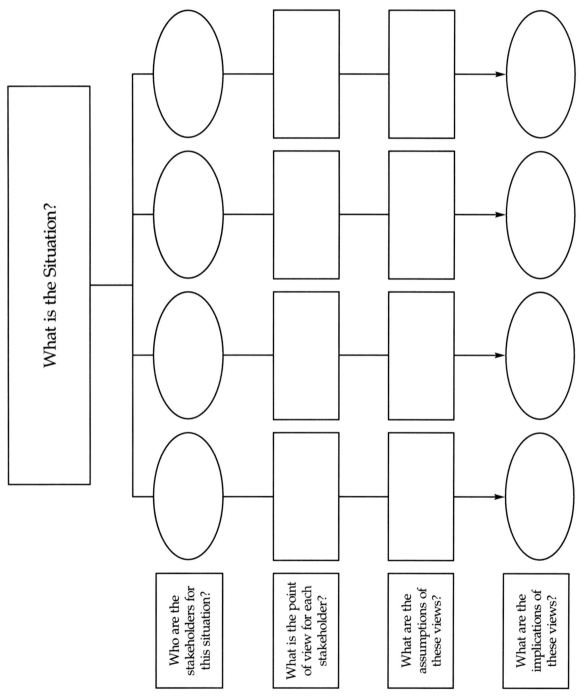

What is the Situation?

Who are the stakeholders for this situation?

What is the point of view for each stakeholder?

What are the assumptions of these views?

What are the implications of these views?

Stockbridge Speech

(From a speech of a member of the Stockbridge tribe to the Massachusetts congress, 1775.)

Brothers! You remember, when you first came over the great waters, I was great and you were little—very small. I then took you in for a friend, and kept you under my arms, so that no one might injure you. Since that time we have ever been true friends: there has never been any quarrel between us. But now our conditions are changed. You are become great and tall. You reach to the clouds. You are seen all around the world. I am become small—very little. I am not so high as your knee. Now you take care of me; and I look to you for protection.

Brothers! I am sorry to hear of this great quarrel between you and old England. It appears that blood must soon be shed to end this quarrel. We never till this day understood the foundation of this quarrel between you and the country you came from. Brothers! Whenever I see your blood running, you will soon find me about to revenge my brothers' blood. Although I am low and very small, I will grip hold of your enemy's heel, that he cannot run so fast, and so light, as if he had nothing at his heels.

Brothers! You know I am not so wise as you are; therefore I ask your advice in what I am now going to say. I have been thinking, before you come to action, to take a run to the westward and feel the mind of my Indian brethren, the Six Nations, and know how they stand—whether they are on your side or for your enemies. If I find they are against you, I will try to turn their minds. I think they will listen to me, for they have always looked this way for advice, concerning all important news that comes from the rising sun. If they hearken to me, you will not be afraid of any danger from behind you. However their minds are affected, you shall soon know by me. . . .

Brothers! One thing I ask you, if you send me to fight: that you will let me fight in my own way. I am not used to the English fashion; therefore you must not expect I can train like your men. Only point out to me where your enemies keep, and that is all I shall want to know.

Source: Bruun and Crosby, *Our Nation's Archive,* p. 123.

Poem to George Washington

SIR,

I have taken the freedom to address your Excellency in the enclosed poem, and entreat your acceptance, though I am not insensible of its inaccuracies. Your being appointed by the Grand Continental Congress to be Generalissimo of the armies of North America, together with the fame of your virtues, excite sensations not easy to suppress. Your generosity, therefore, I presume, will pardon the attempt. Wishing your Excellency all possible success in the great cause you are so generously engaged in, I am,

Your Excellency's most obedient humble servant,
PHYLLIS WHEATLEY

Chorus:

Celestial choir! enthron'd in realms of light,
Columbia's scenes of glorious toils I write.
While freedom's cause her anxious breast alarms,
She flashes dreadful in refulgent arms.
See mother earth her offspring's fate bemoan,
And nations gaze at scenes before unknown!
See the bright beams of heaven's revolving light
Involved in sorrows and the veil of night!

The goddess comes, she moves divinely fair,
Olive and laurel binds her golden hair: . . .
Muse! bow propitious while my pen relates
How pour her armies through a thousand gates: . . .

In bright array they seek the work of war,
Where high unfurl'd the ensign waves in air.
Shall I to Washington their praise recite?
Thee, first in place and honours—we demand
The grace and glory of thy martial band . . .
Proceed, great chief, with virtue on thy side,
Thy ev'ry action let the goddess guide.
A crown, a mansion, and a throne that shine,
With gold unfading, WASHINGTON! be thine.

Source: *http://www.jmu.edu/madison/wheatley/*

Washington's Reply

Cambridge, February 28, 1776

Mrs. Phillis,

... I thank you most sincerely for your polite notice of me, in the elegant Lines you enclosed; and however undeserving I may be of such encomium and panegyrick, the style and manner exhibit a striking proof of your great poetical Talents. In honour of which, and as a tribute justly due to you, I would have published the Poem, had I not been apprehensive, that, while I only meant to give the World this new instance of your genius, I might have incurred the imputation of Vanity. This and nothing else, determined me not to give it place in the public Prints.

If you should ever come to Cambridge, or near Head Quarters, I shall be happy to see a person so favoured by the Muses, and to whom Nature has been so liberal and beneficent in her dispensations.

I am, with great Respect, etc.

Source: *http://www.jmu.edu/madison/wheatley/*

Surrender at Yorktown

Lesson 19

Curriculum Alignment

Goal 1	Goal 2	Goal 3	Goal 4	Goal 5
X	X		X	X

 ## Instructional Purpose

- ◆ To share projects on notable individuals of the Revolutionary period
- ◆ To use maps to understand the movements of American, French, and British forces leading to the standoff at Yorktown in 1781
- ◆ To understand the role of naval forces in bringing the war to a close
- ◆ To analyze primary source documents

 ## Materials

1. Student biography projects
2. Map of Virginia (from atlas or on-line)
3. Yorktown (Handout 19A)
4. Cornwallis Surrenders (Handout 19B)
5. Analyzing Primary Sources (Handout 19C)
6. Washington at the End of the War (Handout 19D)

Vocabulary

capitulation—the act of giving up or surrendering, usually under specified conditions

cease-fire—a truce; a suspension or stopping of hostilities

coup—the sudden overthrow of a government

siege—a military blockade of a city or fortress in order to force it to surrender

surrender—to give oneself up or to relinquish control, as to an enemy

📖 Activities

1. Set up a "Gallery of Greats." Have students set up displays of their biography projects, and allow time for them to browse one another's projects. You may also wish to invite students to dress up as their subjects and invite parents and other classes in to learn about the notable individuals.

2. After projects have been shared, ask students to write a response to the following in their journals: *Before you started your biography project, you wrote about what characteristics you thought made a good leader. Based on your own project and what you learned from classmates' projects, how would you answer that question now? What factors do you think influenced the number of eminent individuals involved in the American Revolution? Was it a* **coincidence** *or were there identifiable causes for their involvement?*

3. Have students look at a map of the state of Virginia (current or historical) with sufficient detail to show the location of Yorktown and the surrounding waterways. Tell students that in 1781, the British Lord Cornwallis marched his army from North Carolina into Virginia, successfully making his way toward the coast where he hoped to be joined by more troops and ships from New York. The British then hoped with such a large army together to attack the American army and win a decisive victory against them.

4. Have students find Yorktown and ask the following questions:

   ♦ *Why do you think Cornwallis chose this location to fortify his troops and wait for reinforcements?*

   ♦ *Why might this be a bad place?*

   ♦ *How would the waterways affect the safety of the spot?*

5. Then explain to students that Washington had also decided to move into Virginia to try to strike a decisive blow. Explain that Washington's plan was to block Cornwallis into Yorktown and conduct a siege until the British surrendered. *How would the waterways affect Washington's plan? What would Washington need in addition to his army to block Cornwallis in?* Explain to students that a French fleet under Admiral de Grasse beat the British fleet into the Chesapeake Bay and was able to block Cornwallis's escape across the York River and prevent more British troops from arriving. Give

students copies of **Yorktown** (Handout 19A) to demonstrate the movements of the armies.

6. Share with students **Cornwallis Surrenders** (Handout 19B) and have them analyze the document using **Analyzing Primary Sources** (Handout 19C). Ask students the following questions:

   ◆ *How do you think Cornwallis felt having to write this letter?*

   ◆ *Where does he place the blame for the loss?*

7. Explain to students that although skirmishes between British and American troops continued until 1783 when the Treaty of Paris was signed, the war effectively ended at Yorktown. Ask students:

   ◆ *What were the implications of the end of the fighting?*

   ◆ *What were some of the major causes of this effect?*

   ◆ *How might Yorktown have turned out differently?*

8. Tell students that after the fighting ended but before the Treaty of Paris was signed, some of the army officers began to be resentful of Congress because they had not received all of their promised salary and benefits, among other grievances. Explain that some of the officers were considering rebelling against the Congress, in a military coup. Share with students the first document on **Washington at the End of the War** (Handout 19D) and explain that Washington gave this speech when he showed up unexpectedly at a meeting of the angry officers. Ask students to think about the following:

   ◆ *What is Washington saying in this speech? Whose authority does it emphasize?*

   ◆ *Why do you think Washington's speech was influential to the officers? What does that show about their opinions of him?*

   ◆ *Why is this speech from Washington important? What does it demonstrate about his assumptions about government? What does it demonstrate about Washington's leadership?*

   ◆ *What are the implications if there is great tension between a civil authority, like the Continental Congress, and the military it funds?*

9. Explain that the military crisis was averted, and Washington resigned his commission as general in December 1783 after

the Treaty was signed to return to Mount Vernon. Have students read the second excerpt on their handout, and ask the following questions:

- *Why was Washington's resignation significant? Did Washington have to resign? What else could he have done?*

- *What does Washington's resignation show about his commitment (and the commitment of others around him) to the authority of Congress and the American people? What does it demonstrate about Washington's leadership?*

- *Was this really the end of Washington's "public life"? Why?*

Journal

Ebenezer Denny, a Continental Army officer from Pennsylvania, wrote in his journal that he watched a British drummer signaling each time the messages were carried back and forth from Cornwallis to Washington. When the agreed-upon cease-fire happened, Denny wrote,

The constant firing was too much for the sound of a single drum; but when the firing ceased, I thought I never heard a drum equal to it— the most delightful music to us all.

What do you think Denny meant by his comments? Why was the music of the drum so delightful?

Homework

Review the contents of your unit notebook for a post-assessment in the next lesson.

Note to Teacher

This lesson will require more than one class period with the project presentations.

Assessment

- Individual biography projects
- Primary source analysis
- Participation in discussion
- Journal response

Yorktown

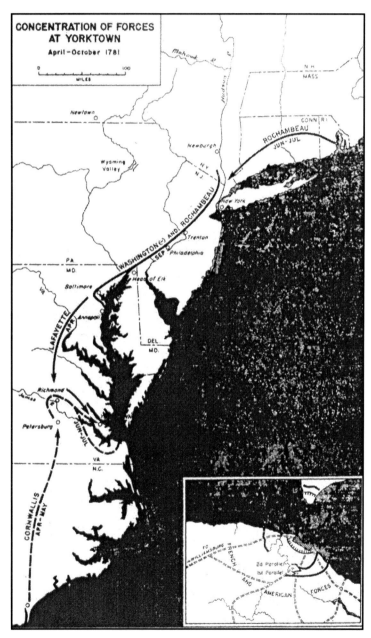

Source: University of Texas PCL Map Collection,
http://www.lib.utexas.edu/maps/histus.html.

Name_____ Date _____

Cornwallis Surrenders

(From Lord Cornwallis's letter to General Henry Clinton in New York after the surrender at Yorktown.)

York Town, Virginia, October 20, 1781

Sir, I have the mortification to inform your Excellency that I have been forced to give up the posts of York and Gloucester, and to surrender the troops under my command, by capitulation on the 19th inst. as prisoners of war to the combined forces of America and France.

I never saw this post in a very favourable light, but when I found I was to be attacked in it in so unprepared a state, by so powerful an army and artillery, nothing but the hopes of relief would have induced me to attempt its defence; for I would either have endeavoured to escape to New-York . . . immediately on the arrival of General Washington's troops at Williamsburgh, or I would . . . have attacked them in the open field. . . . But being assured by your Excellency's letters, that every possible means would be tried by the army and navy to relieve us, I could not think myself at liberty to venture upon either of those desperate attempts. . . .

[After many days of siege,] our numbers [were] diminished by the enemy's fire, but particularly by sickness, and the strength and spirits of those in the works were much exhausted by the fatigue of constant watching and unremitting duty. I thought it would have been wanton and inhuman to the last degree to sacrifice the lives of this small body of gallant soldiers, who had ever behaved with so much fidelity and courage. . . . I therefore proposed to capitulate, and I have the honour to enclose to your Excellency the copy of the correspondence between General Washington and me on that subject, and the terms of capitulation agreed upon. . . .

Source: Rhodehamel, *The American Revolution*, pp. 744–749.

From Center for Gifted Education, *The World Turned Upside Down: The American Revolution.* Copyright © 2003 Kendall/Hunt Publishing Company—may be reproduced by individual teachers for classroom use only.

Analyzing Primary Sources

Document Title:_____

Establishing a Context and Intent for the Source

Author:

Time (When was it written)?

Briefly describe the culture of the time and list related events of the time.

Purpose (Why was the document created?)

Audience (Who was the document created for?)

Understanding the Source

What problems/issues/events does the source address?

What are the main points/ideas/arguments?

What assumptions/values/feelings does the author reflect?

What actions/outcomes does the author expect? From whom?

Evaluating/Interpreting the Source

Authenticity/Reliability (Could the source be invented, edited, or mistranslated? What corroborating evidence do you have about the source? Does the author know enough about the topic to discuss it?)

Representative (How typical is the source of others of the same period? What other information might you need to find this out?)

What could the consequences of this document be? (What would happen if the author's plans were carried out? What could happen to the author when people read this? How might this document affect or change public opinions?)

What were the actual consequences? What really happened as a result of this document?

Short-term

Long-term

What new or different interpretation does this source provide about the historical period?

Washington at the End of the War

(From speech to his officers, March 15, 1783, referring to two anonymous letters sent out suggesting that the officers raise a revolt against Congress or move as a group to the wilderness, abandoning the new nation to defend itself.)

. . . It is calculated to impress the mind, with an idea of premeditated injustice in the Sovereign power of the United States, and rouse all the resentments which must unavoidably flow from such a belief. . . . The way is plain, says the anonymous Addresser. If War continues, remove into the unsettled Country; there establish yourselves, and leave an undefended Country to defend itself. . . . This dreadful alternative, of either deserting our Country in the extremest hour of her distress, or turning our Arms against it, has something so shocking in it, that humanity revolts at the idea. . . . What can this writer have in view, by recommending such measures? Can he be a friend to the Army? Can he be a friend to this Country? Rather, is he not some insidious Foe? . . .

Let me request you to rely on the plighted faith of your Country, and place a full confidence in the purity of the intentions of Congress; that . . . they will cause all your Accounts to be fairly liquidated. . . .

Let me conjure you, in the name of our common Country, as you value your own sacred honor, as you respect the rights of humanity, and as you regard the Military and National character of America, to express your utmost horror and detestation of the Man who wished, under any specious pretences, to overturn the liberties of our Country, and who wickedly attempts to open the flood gates of Civil discord, and deluge our rising Empire in Blood. By thus determining . . . you will give one more distinguished proof of unexampled patriotism and patient virtue. . . .

(From Washington's speech to Congress, December 23, 1783.)

The great events on which my resignation depended, having at length taken place, I have now the honor of offering my sincere congratulations to Congress, and of presenting myself before them, to surrender into their hands the trust committed to me, and to claim the indulgence of retiring from the service of my country. . . .

The successful termination of the war has verified the most sanguine expectations; and my gratitude for the interposition of Providence, and the assistance I have received from my country-men, increases with every review of the momentous contest. . . .

Having now finished the work assigned me, I retire from the great theatre of action, and bidding an affectionate farewell to this august body, under whose orders I have so long acted, I here offer my commission, and take my leave of all the employments of public life.

Source: Rhodehamel, *The American Revolution.*

The World Turned Upside Down

Curriculum Alignment

Goal 1	Goal 2	Goal 3	Goal 4	Goal 5
X	X	X	X	X

Instructional Purpose

+ To explore the implications of the end of the Revolutionary War for Americans, the British, and for others around the world
+ To trace the influence of the Revolution on ideas and actions in the years following

Materials/Resources

1. The World Turned Upside Down (Handout 20A)
2. What Next? (Handout 20B)
3. American Revolution Post-Assessment (Handout 20C)
4. American Revolution Assessment Scoring Guide (Teacher Resource 20)
5. Cause and Effect Model (Handout 20D)

Vocabulary

revolution—the overthrow of a government to replace it with another; a momentous change in a situation or cultural context

Activities

1. Share with students the lyrics (and a recording if possible) of **The World Turned Upside Down** (Handout 20A). Tell students that this music was played as the British soldiers marched past the French and American troops after the surrender at Yorktown. Ask students the following questions:

   + *What are the words of this song referring to? How is it similar to the song "The Rich Lady over the Sea" you read earlier?*

- *How do you think the British soldiers felt, surrendering to the Americans and French with this song being played?*

- *What do you think is the meaning of the title of the song?*

2. Remind students of the Emerson poem they read in Lesson 7 and the line referring to "The shot heard 'round the world." Ask students why they think the events of the Revolution were seen as significant "'round the world," and why it turned things "upside down." Explore the term *revolution* with students. Encourage them to find the stems of the word and related terms such as *revolve,* and emphasize the different meanings related to *turning* and to *change.* Ask students how these meanings relate to the use of the term in social and political situations. Give students the following definition: *The overthrow of one government and its replacement with another.* Explain that usually revolutions involve class conflicts, emphasis on greater economic freedoms, and major social reforms. Ask students the following questions:

- *In what ways does this definition apply to the American Revolution? In what ways does it not apply?*

- *Why do you think some historians and writers prefer the term "War for Independence" instead of "American Revolution"?*

3. Share with students the following quote, written by Benjamin Rush after the battle of Yorktown: *"The American war is over, but that is far from being the case with the American Revolution. On the contrary, nothing but the first act of the great drama is closed."* Ask students to discuss what they think this statement means, either orally or in their journals. Then distribute copies of **What Next?** (Handout 20B) and have students work in groups to think about the implications of the end of the war. Have students share their group responses to the sheet.

4. Distribute the **American Revolution Post-Assessment** (Handout 20C) and have students complete.

Homework

Review the generalizations on the **Cause and Effect Model** (Handout 20D). Fill in the model with examples from your study of the American Revolution that support each generalization.

Extension

The French Revolution, which began in 1789, was a more classic example of a revolution than the American war. Find out about the type of government the French had before their Revolution and the types of government that followed it.

Assessment

◆ Responses to discussion and chart
◆ Post-assessment

Notes

The World Turned Upside Down

Goody Bull and her daughter together fell out,

Both squabbled and wrangled and made a great rout.

But the cause of the quarrel remains to be told,

Then lend both your ears and a tale I'll unfold.

Derry down, down, hey derry down.

Then lend both your ears and a tale I'll unfold.

The old lady, it seems, took a freak in her head,

That her daughter, grown woman, might earn her own bread,

Self-applauding her scheme, she was ready to dance,

But we're often too sanguine in what we advance.

Derry down, down, hey derry down.

But we're often too sanguine in what we advance.

For mark the event, thus for fortune we're crossed,

Nor should people reckon without their good host,

The daughter was sulky and wouldn't come to,

And pray what in this case could the old woman do?

Derry down, down, hey derry down.

And pray what in this case could the old woman do? . . .

Source: McNeil and McNeil, *Colonial and Revolutionary Songbook*, p. 49.

What Next?

Fill in the chart with some possible implications of the end of the war for each of the people or groups listed.

Continental Congress	Parliament
Continental Army	**British Army**
Citizens of the United States	Loyalists in the United States
Legislatures of each of the individual states	Citizens of other countries dissatisfied with their governments

Name_____ Date _____

American Revolution
Post-Assessment

Circle the BEST response to each question.

1. Which of these was NOT a reason why Congress chose George Washington to be commander in chief of the Continental Army?
   a. Washington applied for the job.
   b. Washington was not from New England.
   c. Washington had experience in the army.
   d. Washington was the only candidate seriously considered for the job.

2. What was the main reason for the colonial opposition to the Stamp Act?
   a. Taxes under the Stamp Act would put a large financial burden on the colonists.
   b. The Stamp Act was the first major tax imposed by Great Britain on the colonies.
   c. The Stamp Act emphasized to colonists that they did not have a voice in Parliament.
   d. Taxes collected under the Stamp Act would not provide any benefits for the colonies.

3. Which of the following statements was NOT one of the purposes of the Declaration of Independence?
   a. To identify the actions of the king that the colonists felt were unjust
   b. To apply a philosophy about people's natural rights to the colonial situation
   c. To outline details for a new system of government for the colonies
   d. To show official commitment to the Revolutionary movement

4. Which of the following was the most important factor influencing the start of the fighting in the Revolution?
   a. Tensions stirred up in New England by radical colonists opposing British actions
   b. British movement of troops into the major ports of New York, Philadelphia, and Charleston
   c. The Continental Congress's decision to declare independence from Great Britain
   d. Thomas Paine's pamphlet *Common Sense* saying the colonies should be free from Britain

5. Which of these statements is true about African American participation in the Revolutionary War?

   a. African Americans were not allowed to fight in the Continental Army because Southern leaders were afraid of slave revolts.

   b. British military leaders promised African American slaves their freedom if they ran away from their masters to fight for the king.

   c. All African Americans in this period were slaves, so they could only fight if their masters sent them to the army or if they ran away.

   d. Most African Americans supported the British because they believed the British could offer them a better life in the West Indies.

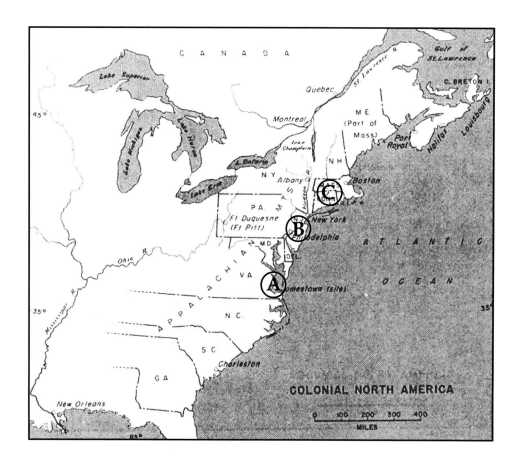

6. Look at the map. Which set of letters shows the order in which most of the fighting progressed?

   a. ABC

   b. BCA

   c. CAB

   d. CBA

7. Which of the following factors contributed MOST to the American victory in the War for Independence?

   a. Support for the war from the majority of the American people

   b. Major American victories in battle at Bunker Hill, Saratoga, and Valley Forge

   c. Financial and military support for the Americans from France

   d. Military superiority of the American troops

8. Which of these statements is the best explanation of this description of governments from the Declaration of Independence: "deriving their just powers from the consent of the governed"?

   a. The purpose of a government is to pass laws and to make sure that the laws are followed.

   b. Government has authority over people because the people agree to give authority to the government.

   c. People have unalienable rights to life, liberty, and property, and governments must protect those rights.

   d. The king of England was unjust to the colonists, so he should not have governmental power.

9. Which of these pairs of statements shows an accurate cause and effect relationship?

   a. George Washington was appointed commander in chief of the army, so the American troops drove the British from Lexington and Concord back to Boston.

   b. Five colonists were killed in the Boston Massacre, so the Sons of Liberty dumped the British tea into the harbor in the Boston Tea Party.

   c. The Continental Congress voted to accept the Virginia Resolutions, so Thomas Jefferson wrote the Declaration of Independence.

   d. The Continental Army showed its ability to win at Saratoga, so the French government signed a treaty of alliance with the United States.

10. Put the following events into the order in which they happened. Place a **1** beside the earliest event, a **2** beside the second event, and so on.

   _____ The Boston Tea Party

   _____ The Battle of Bunker Hill

   _____ The Battle of Saratoga

   _____ The signing of the Declaration of Independence

   _____ The Tea Act

Write your responses to each of the questions below.

11. Choose one of these acts of Parliament. Explain what the act said, why Parliament passed it, and what some of its effects were.
    ◆ The Stamp Act
    ◆ The Tea Act
    ◆ The Quartering Act

    _____

    _____

    _____

    _____

    _____

12. Select two of the following individuals. For each one, explain who the person was and why he or she was important in the Revolutionary period.
    ◆ Thomas Paine
    ◆ Abigail Adams
    ◆ Benjamin Franklin
    ◆ Lord Cornwallis

    _____

    _____

    _____

    _____

    _____

13. List and explain two causes of the American Revolution.

_____

_____

_____

_____

_____

14. Describe two different roles that women played during the Revolutionary War. For each role, explain how it was a change for women from their lives before the war.

_____

_____

_____

_____

_____

Read the excerpt below, from a speech given by Patrick Henry to the Virginia Assembly in March of 1775, and answer the questions.

> If we wish to be free ... we must fight! I repeat it, sir, we must fight! They tell us, sir, that we are weak; unable to cope with so formidable an adversary. But when shall we be stronger? Will it be the next week, or the next year? Will it be when we are totally disarmed, and when a British guard shall be stationed in every house? ...
>
> Gentlemen may cry, Peace, Peace—but there is no peace. The war is actually begun! The next gale that sweeps from the north will bring to our ears the clash of resounding arms! Our brethren are already in the field! Why stand we here idle?

What is it that gentlemen wish? What would they have? Is life so dear, or peace so sweet, as to be purchased at the price of chains and slavery? Forbid it, Almighty God! I know not what course others may take; but as for me, give me liberty or give me death!

15. What is the purpose of the speech?

_____

_____

_____

_____

16. Name two implications Patrick Henry suggests of not supporting his point of view.

_____

_____

_____

_____

17. Explain in your own words the statement "Give me liberty or give me death" and how it applied to Patrick Henry's situation.

_____

_____

_____

_____

American Revolution Assessment
Scoring Guide

Circle the BEST response to each question.

1. a.

2. c.

3. c.

4. a.

5. b.

6. d.

7. c.

8. b.

9. d.

Scoring for questions 1–9:

Score 2 points for each correct response.

Score 0 points for each incorrect response.

10. Put the following events into the order in which they happened. Place a 1 beside the earliest event, a 2 beside the second event, and so on.

_2_ The Boston Tea Party

_3_ The Battle of Bunker Hill

_5_ The Battle of Saratoga

_4_ The signing of the Declaration of Independence

_1_ The Tea Act

Scoring for question 10:

Score 4 points if all five events are correctly numbered.

Score 2 points if at least three consecutive events are grouped together in the correct order but not all five.

Score 1 point if two consecutive events are grouped together in the correct order.

Score 0 points if none of the above criteria apply.

Write your responses to each of the questions below.

11. Choose one of these Acts of Parliament. Explain what the act said, why Parliament passed it, and what some of its effects were.

- The Stamp Act
- The Tea Act
- The Quartering Act

Possible responses include *the Stamp Act required colonists to pay for official stamps on many different types of documents, Parliament passed it to help bring in funds to pay for the expenses from the French and Indian War, colonists reacted against it because they felt they had no say in it, colonies came together in Stamp Act Congress and protested it; the Tea Act put a tax on tea for the colonies but allowed the British East India Company to undersell colonial merchants, Parliament hoped to support the East India Company, the colonists protested and boycotted the tea, the Boston Tea Party occurred; the Quartering Act required colonists to quarter British troops or take them into their homes and feed them, Parliament passed it to protect the colonists from hostile Indians but also to keep watch on the colonists and to provide shelter for troops, colonists reacted against it and used it as a basis for protest with other acts.*

Scoring for question 11:

*Score **4** points if response identifies an act, its purpose, and at least one clearly related effect.*

*Score **2** points if response identifies an act and makes an attempt to demonstrate Parliament's purpose and/or a related effect.*

*Score **0** points if none of the above criteria apply.*

12. Select two of the following individuals. For each one, explain who the person was and why he or she was important in the Revolutionary period.

- Thomas Paine
- Abigail Adams
- Benjamin Franklin
- Lord Cornwallis

Possible responses include *Thomas Paine was an Englishman living in the colonies who wrote the pamphlet Common Sense encouraging the colonies to declare independence, his writings were very popular and influenced political decision-making during the Revolution; Abigail Adams was the wife of John Adams,* one of the prominent members of the Continental Congress, her letters to her husband and his letters to her show reactions to major events of the time, she encouraged her husband to remember the importance of rights for women as well as men; Benjamin Franklin was a leading supporter of colonial independence and a member of the committee that prepared the Declaration of Independence, he went to France as a representative of the colonies for much of the war and helped ensure the French-American alliance; Lord Cornwallis was a British Army general who was very successful against the Americans especially in the Southern states toward the end of the war, he was planning to join with forces from New York to strike a major blow to the Continental Army in Virginia but was boxed in by the French and Americans and surrendered at Yorktown, basically ending the war.

Scoring for question 12:

Score 4 points if response identifies two individuals correctly with at least one key detail for each.

Score 2 points if response identifies one individual correctly with at least one key detail.

Score 0 points if none of the above criteria apply.

13. List and explain two causes of the American Revolution.

Possible responses include *colonial opposition to taxation, with colonists protesting taxation without representation and the types of taxes and restrictions passed; public attention to radical colonial groups who promoted ideas of independence and took positions of leadership to further those ideas; tensions between colonists and British troops stationed in the colonies that escalated into violence; economic opportunities for the colonies that would increase without British restrictions on trade; philosophies of government that suggested possibilities for different directions for the colonies.*

Scoring for question 13:

Score 4 points if response identifies two valid causes of the Revolution AND provides elaboration on why each was an issue.

Score 2 points if response identifies two valid causes of the Revolution and provides elaboration on at least one.

Score 1 point if response identifies and explains one valid cause.

Score 0 points if none of the above criteria apply.

14. Describe two different roles that women played during the Revolutionary War. For each role, explain how it was a change for women from their lives before the war.

Possible responses include *taking on work at home formerly done by men; being "camp followers" and traveling with the army to cook, clean, carry water, and help with the sick; fighting in battle in disguise as men; being spies; opening their homes to house troops.*

Scoring for question 14:

*Score **4** points if response identifies at least two roles and how they caused change.*

*Score **2** points if response identifies at two roles but does not provide explanation of change.*

*Score **1** point if response identifies one role.*

*Score **0** points if none of the above criteria apply.*

Read the excerpt below, from a speech given by Patrick Henry to the Virginia Assembly in March of 1775, and answer the questions.

If we wish to be free … we must fight! I repeat it, sir, we must fight! They tell us, sir, that we are weak; unable to cope with so formidable an adversary. But when shall we be stronger? Will it be the next week, or the next year? Will it be when we are totally disarmed, and when a British guard shall be stationed in every house? …

Gentlemen may cry, Peace, Peace—but there is no peace. The war is actually begun! The next gale that sweeps from the north will bring to our ears the clash of resounding arms! Our brethren are already in the field! Why stand we here idle? What is it that gentlemen wish? What would they have? Is life so dear, or peace so sweet, as to be purchased at the price of chains and slavery? Forbid it, Almighty God! I know not what course others may take; but as for me, give me liberty or give me death!

15. What is the purpose of the speech? What evidence supports your response?

Possible responses include *to raise support in the Assembly for the Patriot cause, to encourage a sense of connection with rising tensions in Massachusetts, to predict possibilities for the future if colonists did not act, to convince the Assembly of the seriousness of the situation between the colonies and Britain.*

Scoring for question 15:

*Score **4** points if response clearly identifies and supports at least one purpose of the speech.*

*Score **2** points if response identifies a valid purpose and makes an attempt to support.*

*Score **0** points if none of the above criteria apply.*

16. Name two implications Patrick Henry suggests of not supporting his point of view.

   Possible responses include *weapons and ways of defending themselves taken away from the colonies, British troops stationed in every house in the colonies, increased restrictions on life in the colonies.*

Scoring for question 16:

*Score **4** points if response clearly identifies two valid implications from the speech.*

*Score **2** points if response clearly identifies one valid implication from the speech.*

*Score **0** points if none of the above criteria apply.*

17. Explain in your own words the statement "Give me liberty or give me death" and how it applied to Patrick Henry's situation.

   Possible responses include *freedom or liberty is the most important thing in life to me, I would rather lose my life than live without freedom, liberty is more important than anything else in life; Patrick Henry believed the situation between the colonies and Great Britain had reached a point of no return, that either the colonists had to fight for their freedom, live in "slavery," or die, he was pledging his life to the cause of liberty for the colonies, he wanted the members of the Virginia Assembly to pledge their lives to the fight.*

Scoring for question 17:

*Score **4** points if response explains the words and the context of the quote clearly.*

*Score **2** points if response explains the words of the quote and attempts to relate it to Henry's situation.*

*Score **0** points if none of the above criteria apply.*

Cause and Effect Model

Give 2 to 3 examples for each generalization that show how the generalization is true.

Causes may have predictable and unpredictable effects.	Causes can trigger simple effects or chains of related effects.
An effect can be the result of multiple causes with different degrees of influence.	A relationship between events that seems to be cause-effect may actually be correlational or coincidental.
Causes have short-term and long-term effects.	Hindsight and new discoveries can help us to understand past cause and effect relationships.

Implementation
Guidelines

P
a
r
t

III

Implementation Guidelines

The following pages outline some guidelines for teachers in implementing this unit effectively in classrooms, including some design and logistical discussions and outlines of the central teaching models. Feedback from teachers who piloted the unit has been used in developing these recommendations.

Target Population

This unit was designed to serve the learning needs of highly able students in the upper elementary grades (grades 4–5). Lessons have been piloted both in classes for the gifted and in heterogeneous settings, with teachers modifying some reading selections and activities for use with some students as appropriate.

Alignment of the Unit with Standards

The unit was designed to align with U.S. History standards of the *Standards of Learning for Virginia Public Schools* (Commonwealth of Virginia Department of Education, 2001). The unit also aligns with the standards set forth by the National Center for History in the Schools and the National Council for the Social Studies, with regard to both process and content elements, including emphases on chronological thinking and historical analysis and interpretation. The unit also supports student learning in other areas, particularly in the language arts area of persuasive writing.

Schedule for Unit Implementation

Many of the lessons incorporated in this unit will require more than one class period to implement. Indications are provided in some lessons as to appropriate points at which to split the lesson. Because of the heavy reading and writing emphasis, many lessons may be accomplished through incorporating activities across both language arts and social studies sessions. The unit is designed to represent approximately 4 to 6 weeks of instruction.

Use of Technology

Internet access and other technological tools will provide support for unit implementation and enhance the experience for students and teachers. Some relevant sites are noted in the unit lessons and resources. In addition, the Internet is a useful resource for completing the unit projects. Beyond this, computers should be utilized to support student word-processing skills on writing assignments in the unit, and presentation software may be used in project development.

Collaboration with Media Specialists

Teachers and media specialists can work together to collect the necessary resources for the unit and have them available in the classroom or media center during implementation. Some of the resources recommended in this unit may not be available at school libraries but may be found in public or university libraries, and specialists at these institutions can be very helpful as well in collecting listed resources and recommending additional ones.

Students should also be encouraged to utilize their library/media centers and to become acquainted with the librarians in their community for several reasons. First, libraries are complex systems of organizing information. The systems vary from one library to another, and technological access to the systems is constantly changing. Librarians serve as expert guides to the information maze, and they are eager to assist library users. Secondly, the most important skill in using the library is knowing how to ask questions. Students should learn that working with a librarian is not a one-time inquiry or plea for assistance, but an interactive communication and discovery process. As the student asks a question and the librarian makes suggestions, the student will gain a better understanding of the topic and find new questions and ideas to explore. To maximize the use of library resources, the student should then discuss these new questions and ideas with the librarian. Learning to use the services of librarians and other information professionals is an important tool for lifelong learning.

Learning Centers

Learning centers can serve as useful tools throughout this unit, to give students more opportunities to explore the topics of the unit and to deepen their understanding. A few suggestions for learning centers are outlined below.

The American Revolution Center

At this center, various background resources on the Revolution and artifacts of the culture of the time may be available for students to explore. Historical fiction selections, poetry, art prints, audio recordings of music, and films about the Revolution (both documentary and feature) may be provided, and students may respond to specific questions or provide their own questions and ideas for others to answer. You may wish to make this center a responsibility for groups of students to maintain during the unit, with each group having responsibility to suggest resources, questions, and activities for the center, based on their individual research projects.

Writing Center

Students may work at a writing center to strengthen their persuasive writing skills throughout the unit. They may use the writing center to revise and edit assignments given in the lessons, or to practice writing in response to other prompts provided. Copies of the Hamburger Model should be available at the writing center for students' reference.

Computer Center

A computer center may be used in several different ways during the unit. First, students may use computer time for writing and editing or for working on their research projects for the unit. In addition, relevant websites may be bookmarked for students to visit and explore; some sites are listed in the resources section.

Primary Source Analysis Center

At this center, additional primary sources beyond those used in the unit, including pictures and maps from the time as well as written documents, may be available for students to study. The primary source analysis chart used in the unit may be used at the center as well, along with other resources for primary source analysis such as those provided by the National Archives (see *http://www.nara.gov/ education/teaching/analysis/analysis.html*). Some resources for primary sources are listed in the resource section of the unit.

Map Center

At this center, the emphasis should be on exploring maps of key areas and events created both at the time of and after the Revolution. Students should have opportunities to explore battle maps, political maps, and physical maps to help them gain an understanding of how geography affected the events of the war.

Key Events for Unit Timeline

The following list includes some of the major events of the Revolutionary period that should appear on students' individual unit timelines and a class timeline to be posted during the unit. The list is not intended to be exhaustive, and students may add other events to their timelines as they discover details about the period.

1763:	End of French and Indian War
1764:	Sugar Act passed
1765:	Quartering Act passed
1765:	Stamp Act passed (March)
1765:	Stamp Act Resolutions (October)
1766:	Stamp Act repealed (March)
1766:	Declaratory Act passed
1767:	Townshend Acts passed
1770:	Boston Massacre (March)
1773:	Tea Act passed
1773:	Boston Tea Party (December)
1774:	"Intolerable" Acts passed
1774:	First Continental Congress
1775:	Lexington and Concord (April)
1775:	Second Continental Congress convened (May)
1775:	Bunker Hill (June)
1775:	Washington appointed Commander in Chief (June)
1775:	Olive Branch Petition (July)

1776:	*Common Sense* (February)
1776:	Battle at Sullivan's Island (June)
1776:	Declaration of Independence signed (July)
1776:	Battle of Trenton (December)
1777:	Official flag passed (June)
1777:	Battle of Brandywine Creek (September)
1777:	Battle of Saratoga (October)
1777:	Continental Army camps at Valley Forge (December)
1778:	Alliance signed with France (February)
1780:	Battle of Kings Mountain (October)
1781:	Battle of Yorktown (October)
1783:	Treaty of Paris

Teaching Models

The Taba Model for Concept Development

This model is introduced in Lesson 2 of the unit. The concept of cause and effect is used as an organizer throughout the unit, with numerous questions and activities that explore students' understanding of the concept and the generalizations. This model is based on the work of Taba (1962).

The model as described below may be applied with various concepts and with students at various grade and ability levels. The discussion may need additional teacher support; see Lesson 2 for a more extended version of the activity.

Use the following questions to guide an introductory discussion about cause and effect. In groups, students should discuss the questions and record ideas on large sheets of paper for sharing with the class. Each section of the small group activity should be followed by a brief whole-class discussion.

Brainstorm ideas about cause and effect and write down all responses.

♦ *What words come to mind when you think about cause and effect?*

♦ *What are some examples of cause and effect relationships?*

♦ *How do you decide whether something is an example of cause and effect?*

Categorize the ideas that were written down, putting them into groups, and give each group a title.

♦ *How would you categorize these ideas into groups?*

♦ *What could you call each group? Why?*

♦ *Do all of your examples fall into groups? Might some of them belong in more than one group? How else might you group your ideas?*

♦ *What are some of the characteristics of cause and effect, based on the ideas you wrote?*

Brainstorm a list of relationships that are not examples of cause and effect.

- *What are some examples of things that are not cause and effect relationships?*

- *What evidence or proof do you have that these things are not cause and effect?*

- *How might you group the things that are not examples? What can you call each of these groups?*

- *How are the groups of things that are not examples similar to or different from the groups of things that are? Are there patterns to your groupings?*

Make generalizations about cause and effect.

A generalization is something that is always or almost always true. What can you say about cause and effect that is always or almost always true? Use your examples and categories to guide your thinking, and write several statements which are generalizations about cause and effect.

The Hamburger and Dagwood Models for Persuasive Writing

The purpose of the Hamburger and Dagwood Models is to provide students with a useful metaphor to aid them in developing a persuasive paragraph or essay. The model should be introduced by the teacher, showing students that the top bun and the bottom bun represent the introduction and conclusion of any persuasive writing piece. The teacher should note that the reasons given in support of the thesis statement are like the meat or vegetables in a hamburger, providing the major substance of the sandwich. Elaboration represents the condiments in a sandwich—the ketchup, mustard, and onions that hold a sandwich together—just as examples and illustrations hold a persuasive writing piece together. In the more elaborate Dagwood Model, opposing points of view may be addressed and refuted within the essay with the addition of more "meat" to the sandwich.

Teachers should show students examples of persuasive paragraphs and essays and have students find the pieces. Discuss how "good" each sandwich is. Then teachers should ask students to construct their own pieces. After students have constructed their own paragraphs, teachers may use peer and self-assessments to have students judge their own and one another's writing. This process should be repeated throughout the unit.

This unit utilizes the Hamburger Model, but some students may be ready to use the more complex Dagwood Model. Both models are included on the following pages for reference.

Hamburger Model for
Persuasive Writing

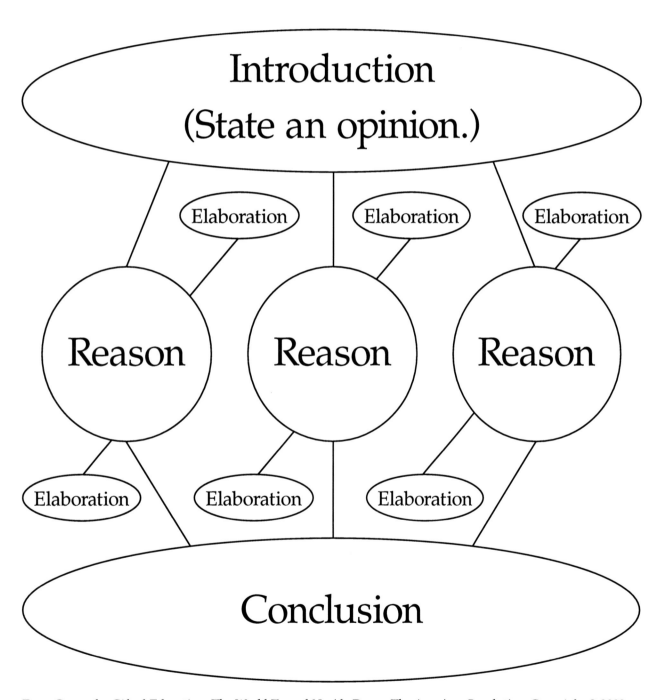

Dagwood Model

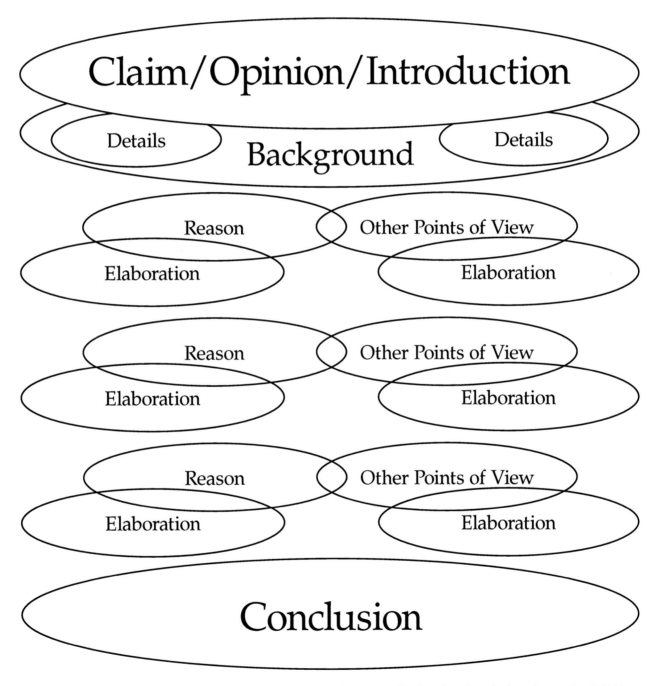

Elements of Reasoning

The reasoning strand used throughout the unit focuses on eight elements of thought identified by Richard Paul (1992). It is embedded in most lessons of the unit through questions, writing assignments, and research work. These elements of thought are the basic building blocks of productive thinking. Working together, they provide a general logic to reasoning. In document interpretation and listening, they help one make sense of the reasoning of the author or speaker. In writing and speaking, they enable authors or speakers to strengthen their arguments.

Students are often asked to distinguish between facts and opinions. However, between pure opinion and hard facts lie reasoned judgements in which beliefs are supported by reasons.

1. **Purpose, Goal, or End in View:** We reason to achieve some objective, to satisfy a desire, or to fulfill some need. For example, if the car does not start in the morning, the purpose of my reasoning is to figure out a way to get to work. One source of problems in reasoning is traceable to "defects" at the level of purpose or goal. If our goal itself is unrealistic, contradictory to other goals we have, or confused or muddled in some way, then the reasoning we use to achieve it is problematic. If we are clear on the purpose for our writing and speaking, it will help focus the message in a coherent direction. The purpose in our reasoning might be to persuade others. When we read and listen, we should be able to determine the author's or speaker's purpose.

2. **Question at Issue (or Problem to Be Solved):** When we attempt to reason something out, there is at least one question at issue or problem to be solved (if not, there is no reasoning required). If we are not clear about what the question or problem is, it is unlikely that we will find a reasonable answer, or one that will serve our purpose. As part of the reasoning process, we should be able to formulate the question to be answered or the issue to be addressed (for example, *Why won't the car start?* or *Should libraries censor materials that contain objectionable language?*).

3. **Points of View or Frame of Reference:** As we take on an issue, we are influenced by our own point of view. For example, parents of young children and librarians might have different points of view on censorship issues. The price of a shirt may seem too low to one person, while it seems high to another because of a different frame of reference. Any defect in our point of view or frame of reference is a possible

source of problems in our reasoning. Our point of view may be too narrow, may not be precise enough, may be unfairly biased, and so forth. By considering multiple points of view, we may sharpen or broaden our thinking. In writing and speaking, we may strengthen our arguments by acknowledging other points of view. In listening and reading, we need to identify the perspective of the speaker or author and understand how it affects the message delivered.

4. **Experiences, Data, and Evidence:** When we reason, we must be able to support our point of view with reasons or evidence. Evidence is important in order to distinguish opinions from reasoned judgement. Evidence and data should support the author's or speaker's point of view and can strengthen an argument. An example is data from surveys or published studies. In reading and listening, we can evaluate the strength of an argument or the validity of a statement by examining the supporting data or evidence. Experiences can also contribute to the data of our reasoning. For example, previous experiences in trying to get a car to start may contribute to the reasoning process that is necessary to solve the problem.

5. **Concepts and Ideas:** Reasoning requires the understanding and use of concepts and ideas, including definitional terms, principles, rules, or theories. When we read and listen, we can ask ourselves, "What are the key ideas presented?" When we write and speak, we can examine and organize our thoughts around the substance of concepts and ideas. Some examples of concepts are *freedom, friendship,* and *responsibility.*

6. **Assumptions:** We need to take some things for granted when we reason. We need to be aware of the assumptions we have made and the assumptions of others. If we make faulty assumptions, this can lead to defects in reasoning. As a writer or speaker, we make assumptions about our audience and our message. For example, we might assume that others will share our point of view, or we might assume that the audience is familiar with the First Amendment when we refer to "First Amendment rights." As a reader or listener, we should be able to identify the assumptions of the writer or speaker.

7. **Inferences:** Reasoning proceeds by steps called *inferences.* An inference is a small step of the mind, in which a person concludes that something is true because of something else being true or seeming to be true. The tentative conclusions (inferences) we make depend on what we assume as we

attempt to make sense of the evidence we see. For example, we see dark clouds and infer that it is going to rain; we know the movie starts at 7:00, and it is now 6:45; it takes 30 minutes to get to the theater; so we cannot get there on time. Many of our inferences are justified and reasonable, but many are not. We need to distinguish between the raw data of our experiences and our interpretations of those experiences (inferences). Also, the inferences we make are heavily influenced by our point of view and assumptions.

8. **Implications and Consequences:** When we reason in a certain direction, we need to look at the consequences of that direction. When we argue and support a certain point of view, solid reasoning requires that we consider what the implications are of following that path. What are the consequences of taking the course that we support? When we read or listen to an argument, we need to ask ourselves what follows from that way of thinking. We can also consider consequences of actions that characters in stories take. For example, if I don't do my homework, I will have to stay after school to do it; if I water the lawn, it will not wither in the summer heat.

Adapted from Paul. R. (1992). *Critical Thinking: What every person needs to survive in a rapidly changing world.* Sonoma, CA: Foundation for Critical Thinking.

Reasoning about a Situation or Event

This model should be used when analyzing a specific event where two or more people or groups of people conflict with one another and have a vested interest in the outcome of the event. This may be the American Constitutional Convention, the Battle of Little Big Horn, the Versailles Treaty proceedings following World War I, a Supreme Court case, a Congressional debate over a specific issue, a community meeting over new zoning laws, or a fight between a parent and a child over missing curfew. This model uses the basic elements and premise of Paul's Reasoning Model, while trying to focus on the various stakeholders in a given situation.

Problem/Situation/Event: The first step is to identify the situation to be analyzed. When using this method of reasoning, it is helpful if the situation is one where groups with multiple viewpoints confront or interact with one another at a specific point in time. The Reasoning about a Situation approach is appropriate when seeking resolution or analyzing why a situation turned out or was resolved in the way it was. An example might be the charge of the U.S. army against Native Americans at Wounded Knee in 1890. **What is the situation to be analyzed? When did it happen? Where?**

Stakeholders: In any situation, there are people or groups of people who have an interest or a stake in the outcome of the situation; they have something to lose or to gain in the situation. These people will, therefore, have some involvement in the situation. When identifying groups of people, being more specific in describing them will make the reasoning process simpler. Following the Wounded Knee example, specifying 7th U.S. Cavalry or the U.S. Army in the West, instead of the U.S. Army (the 7th Cavalry's connection with the defeat at Little Big Horn shaped their point of view, which was not as true for the entire U.S. Army, who may have had little contact with Native American peoples) OR the Sioux or Lakota instead of just Native Americans (Native American peoples in other parts of the U.S. would have had a very different perspective on this event). **Who are the stakeholders in this event?**

Point of View: Each stakeholder has a point of view concerning the situation that must be identified. Identifying a group's point of view may require an investigation of that group's past. For example, it is impossible to describe the point of view of Serbs and Croats in the former Yugoslavia without a knowledge of the centuries of interaction, power struggles, and conflict among those groups. Questions such as: **Why is this group/person a stakeholder?, What does this group/person stand to gain or lose in this situation?, What role does this group/person play in this situation?** can lead to a better understanding of the group's/person's point of view concerning the given situation. **What is each stakeholder's point of view?**

Assumptions: Once the point of view of each stakeholder has been established, the next step is to identify the assumptions each group will hold concerning the situation and the other stakeholders. For example, at Wounded Knee the soldiers may have assumed that the Ghost Dance meant that the Native Americans were going to lead an armed assault to get rid of the whites; they may have assumed that white society was superior to Native societies and therefore should dominate; they may have assumed that Native Americans could not be trusted; they may have assumed that Native Americans were inferior; or they may have assumed that Native Americans were a threat to white society and needed to be subdued or destroyed. Native Americans may have assumed that the soldiers would abide by established codes, such as the white flag of surrender; they may have assumed that through the Ghost Dance, supernatural powers would bring about change on earth; they may have assumed that the U.S. government would communicate with them before sending out the cavalry; or they may have assumed that the cavalry would not charge a village without direct provocation. **What are the assumptions each stakeholder made/will make about the situation, based on their points of view?**

Implications: For each group of stakeholders, what are the implications or possible consequences of their points of view and assumptions for the situation? Look at each stakeholder and identify how the assumptions and point of view will affect the situation. Identify what outcomes each stakeholder wants in the situation, what their assumptions are toward the other groups, and how each stakeholder's views will affect their behavior in the situation. For example, the Lakota at Wounded Knee were not prepared for battle, nor even prepared to flee from an attack. They were participating in a religious movement to return to a former way of life. The soldiers saw Native Americans as inferior and as a threat, and therefore did not feel the need to respect such protocols as the white flag or negotiation. The soldiers also sought to remove the perceived Native American threat through force if necessary. **What are the implications of these assumptions for the situation?**

Interaction: Once the implications of each stakeholder's views have been analyzed, compare and contrast the assumptions and implications of each stakeholder. **What are the implications of these various assumptions interacting? What are potential areas of conflict or compromise in this situation?**

Resolution: **What are the possible resolutions to this situation? What might impede resolution of the situation?**

Reasoning about a Situation or Event

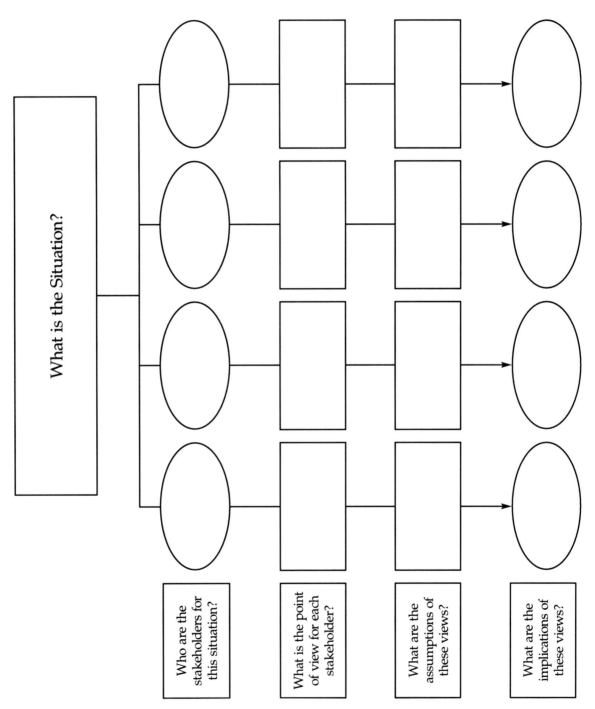

What is the Situation?

Who are the stakeholders for this situation?

What is the point of view for each stakeholder?

What are the assumptions of these views?

What are the implications of these views?

Analyzing Primary Sources

This chart has been developed as a means for teaching students how to confront a historical document, the questions to ask of it, and how to critically examine information they receive.

Document Title. Students should write in the title of the document they are analyzing.

Establishing a Context and Intent for the Source

This section focuses on describing the context out of which the document came. Students should think about several factors in order to gain a fuller understanding of the document.

First, the beliefs, norms, and values of the period that the created the document need to be considered. For example, while today we feel that slavery is wrong, a Southerner in the early nineteenth century may not have agreed. Students need to remember that what we value or think is normal now is not the same as how people viewed the world in the past. Also, students need to think about what other events, developments, or opinions concerning this issue were going on at the time the document was created. Questions to help explore the culture of the time:

- Who does/doesn't have the power?
- Who/What is or isn't important to people at this time?
- What do people believe/hope for/value?
- Was this a new issue, an on-going one, one that was being heatedly debated at the time, or one in which few people were interested?
- What are the major events or trends at the time this document was written?
- Can you think of similar or opposite events that you have read about or studied in class from this time period?

Once students have established a context for the document, the next step is to focus more on the document itself. The students need to examine the intent or **PURPOSE** of the document.

- Why did the author take the time to write this?
- Did a specific event or sentiment of the time trigger this document? Did the author experience something personally that led him or her to write this?
- Was the person required to or asked to write this?
- How might this purpose affect the document?
- What should we watch out for when reading the document?

Tied to purpose is the **AUDIENCE**. The same author may write very differently to different groups of people. For example, there exist accounts of slavery taken from the same person that are completely different because one audience was African American and the other audience was white. The audience can affect the interpretation of the document.

- Who was the document created for?
- How might the audience affect the document?

Understanding the Source

Once students have been alerted to the many factors affecting and shaping the document, they can move on to analyzing what the document is saying.

The first two steps focus on identifying the main ideas of the document. The third question ties back to the context of the document.

- What **assumptions/values/feelings** are reflected in the document?
- What are the author's views about the issue?
- Is the author sympathetic or critical?
- Is the author an insider or outsider to the issue? Is the author personally involved with the issue or is he/she observing others?

Finally, the author had a purpose for writing this and, therefore, must expect something to happen as a result.

- What actions or outcomes does the author expect?
- Does the author expect people to change their opinion, to take a specific action, or to consider a new idea?
- And who does the author expect to do these things? Who or what groups or people are the audience? For example, is an anti-slavery document trying to get slaves, Northerners, or Southern planters to act?

Evaluating/Interpreting the Source

The last section focuses on identifying the effectiveness of the document both for us in the present and for those in the past. The first two questions focus on how useful the source is for making generalizations or conclusions about past events.

The **AUTHENTICITY/RELIABILITY** of a source helps the student decide whether or not this is document is what it claims or appears to be. Historical documents have passed through many hands before they get to present-day readers. During that time people have edited or translated documents, and in doing so may have altered words or the meaning of the document either by accident or intentionally to reflect their own agendas. In addition, especially now with the rise of the Internet, it is possible that while a document appears to be historical, it could have been created recently. The other issue is whether or not the author is qualified to speak about a given issue or event. For example, you would not go to an eye doctor for a hearing problem. Therefore our sources need to have adequate information and experience with the topic being discussed. Students need to eliminate or identify these factors that may alter the accuracy of the document being analyzed.

- Could the source be invented, edited, or mistranslated?
- What evidence do you have or where do you need look to verify the accuracy of the document?
- What evidence do you have to show that the document was not invented later?
- How reliable is this source?
- Is the author an authority on this issue or does he/she at least have sufficient knowledge to speak on the issue?

How **REPRESENTATIVE** a document is of views of the time requires students to identify the prevalence of the ideas in the document at the time. If the document reflects the ranting of a single individual that no one else agrees with or an extremist group that did not reflect the mainstream feelings, then the document needs to be analyzed or treated differently from something that shares the values and ideas of a sizable portion of society. The ideas written down for the culture and related events of the time can help discuss, in broad terms, how many people might agree or disagree with the ideas in the document.

- Would many, some, or few people have agreed with the ideas in this document?
- How do the ideas in this document compare to the culture/events/context of the period in which it was written?
- How does this source compare with others from the same period? Are there other sources from the time that express similar ideas? Different ideas?
- What other information might you need to find this out?

There are two parts to considering the **CONSEQUENCES** of a document: first, the possible outcomes, and then the actual ones. By considering the possible outcomes, students can see that history is not inevitable and that other possibilities that existed. Students confront the role of the individual in changing history and the potential for the failure of ideas or institutions that we take for granted today, such as the Constitution. In addition, they become more aware of the risks that were often taken by people in the past, speaking out and expressing their ideas.

- What could be the consequences of this document?
- What would happen if the author's plans were carried out?
- What could happen to the author when people read this?
- How might this document affect or change public opinions?
- What really happened as a result of this document?
- How did this document affect people's lives or events at the time? (Short-term)
- How does this document affect us today or at other times in the past? (Long-term)

Finally, the student needs to determine what has been gained from analyzing this document. The **NEW OR DIFFERENT INTER-PRETATION** gained from this document is the ideas or insight that the student will take away from the document and use in their understanding of subsequent experiences, both in history class and in their daily lives.

Analyzing Primary Sources

Document Title:_____

Establishing a Context and Intent for the Source

Author:

Time/When was it written?

Briefly describe the culture of the time and list related events of the time.

Purpose (Why was the document created?)

Audience (Who was the document created for?)

Understanding the Source

What problems/issues/events does the source address?

What are the main points/ideas/arguments?

What assumptions/values/feelings does the author reflect?

What actions/outcomes does the author expect? From whom?

Authenticity/Reliability (Could the source be invented, edited, or mistranslated? What corroborating evidence do you have about the source? Does the author know enough about the topic to discuss it?)

Representative (How typical is the source of others of the same period? What other information might you need to find this out?)

What could the consequences of this document be? (What would happen if the author's plans were carried out? What could happen to the author when people read this? How might this document affect or change public opinions?)

What were the actual consequences? What really happened as a result of this document?

Short-term

Long-term

What new or different interpretation does this source provide about the historical period?

References

Part

IV

Selected Resources

American Revolution Resources

Avi. (1984). *The fighting ground*. New York: Harper Trophy.

Berkin, C. (1975). *Jackdaw No. A31: Women of the American Revolution*. Amawalk. NY: Golden Owl.

Blumer, R., & Sachs, S. (Producers). (1997). *Liberty! The American Revolution* [Documentary video series]. St. Paul, MN: KTCA-TV. (Available from PBS Video, 1320 Braddock Place, Alexandria, VA 22314)

Bobrick, B. (1997). *Angel in the whirlwind: The triumph of the American Revolution*. New York: Penguin.

Collier, J. L., & Collier, C. (1974). *My brother Sam is dead*. New York: Scholastic.

Dutcher, D. C. G. (1999). *A concise history of the American Revolution*. Ft. Washington, PA: Eastern National.

Ellis, J. J. (2000). *Founding brothers: The Revolutionary generation*. New York: Knopf.

Fifes and Drums of Williamsburg. (1996). *Echoes of revolution* [CD]. Williamsburg, VA: Colonial Williamsburg Foundation.

Fisher, D. H. (1995). *Paul Revere's ride*. New York: Oxford University Press.

Fleming, T. (1997). *Liberty! The American Revolution*. New York: Viking.

Harmon, R. (Director). *The crossing* [Television broadcast/video recording]. (Available from A&E Television Networks, *www.AandE.com*).

Holton, W. (1999). *Forced founders: Indians, debtors, slaves, and the making of the American Revolution in Virginia*. Chapel Hill: University of North Carolina Press.

Longfellow, H. W., & Bing, C. (Ill.). (2002). *The midnight ride of Paul Revere*. Brooklyn, NY: Handprint Books.

Martin, J. P., & Scheer, G. F. (Ed.). (1962). *Private Yankee Doodle: Being a narrative of some of the adventures, dangers and sufferings of a Revolutionary soldier*. Ft. Washington, PA: Eastern Acorn Press.

McCullough, D. (2001). *John Adams*. New York: Simon & Schuster.

McNeil, K., & McNeil, R. (1996). *Colonial and Revolution songbook*. Riverside, CA: WEM Records.

McNeil, K., & McNeil, R. (1989). *Colonial and Revolution songs*. [Cassette and CD]. Riverside, CA: WEM Records.

Meltzer, M. (1987). *The American revolutionaries: A history in their own words*. New York: Crowell.

O'Dell, S. (1980). *Sarah Bishop*. New York: Scholastic.

Rhodehamel, J. (Ed.). (2001). *The American Revolution: Writings from the War of Independence*. New York: Literary Classics of the United States.

Smith, W. (1988). *Flags to color from the American Revolution*. Santa Barbara, CA: Bellerophon Books.

Trussell, J. B. B., Jr. (1998). *Birthplace of an army: A study of the Valley Forge encampment*. Harrisburg, PA: Pennsylvania Historical and Museum Commission.

General Resources

Bruun, E., & Crosby, J. (Eds.) (1999). *Our nation's archive: The history of the United States in documents.* New York: Black Dog & Leventhal.

Gordon, I. L. (1989). *American history* (2nd ed.). New York: Amsco.

Merriam-Webster's collegiate dictionary (10th ed.). (1993). Springfield, MA: Merriam-Webster.

Monk, L. R. (Ed.). (1994). *Ordinary Americans: U.S. history through the eyes of everyday people.* Alexandria, VA: Close Up.

The American Heritage dictionary of the English language (3rd ed.). (1992). New York: Houghton Mifflin.

Tindall, G. B., & Shi, D. E. (1999). *America: A narrative history* (5th ed.). New York: Norton.

Internet Resources

General Resources

http://ahp.gatech.edu/hisdocs.html [historical documents]

http://memory.loc.gov/ammem/bdsds/bdsdhome.html [Library of Congress timeline]

http://www.hillsdale.edu/academics/history/Documents/War/EMAmRev.htm [documents]

http://www.historyplace.com/unitedstates/revolution/ [general site]

http://www.history.org [Colonial Williamsburg]

http://www.ushistory.org [Independence Hall Association]

http://www.pbs.org/ktca/liberty/index.html [from PBS documentary series Liberty!]

http://www.nara.gov/education/teaching/analysis/analysis.html [National Archives activities]

http://revolution.h-net.msu.edu/ [general site]

http://dlar.libertynet.org/resources.html [David Library of the American Revolution]

http://www.cr.nps.gov/museum/exhibits/revwar/index1.html [National Park Service site]

http://americanrevolution.org [general site]

http://theamericanrevolution.org/index.htm [general site]

Battles and Military History

http://theamericanrevolution.org/battles.asp [general listing]

http://www.masshist.org/bh/ [Bunker Hill]

http://www.ccpl.org/ccl/ftmoultrie.html [Sullivan's Island]

http://www.schistory.org/displays/RevWar/CarolinaDay/battle.html [Sullivan's Island]

http://www.barracks.org/barracks/index.html [Trenton]

http://www.pbs.org/ktca/liberty/chronicle/episode3.html [Trenton]

http://www.ushistory.org/valleyforge/ [Valley Forge]

http://www.valleyforgemuseum.org/index.html [Valley Forge]

http://www.pbs.org/ktca/liberty/chronicle/episode4.html [Saratoga]

http://battle1777.saratoga.org/ [Saratoga]

http://www.brandywine225.com/ [Brandywine]

http://www.ushistory.org/march/phila/brandywine.htm [Brandywine]

http://jrshelby.com/kimocowp/km.htm [Kings Mountain]

http://www.wilkesnc.org/history/ovta.htm [Kings Mountain]
http://xenophongroup.com/mcjoynt/yrkcam-z.htm [Yorktown]
http://www.nps.gov/colo/Ythanout/ytbriefs.html [Yorktown]

Maps

http://www.lib.utexas.edu/maps/histus.html [Univ. of Texas Perry-Castaneda Map
    Collection]
http://www.earlyamerica.com/earlyamerica/maps/yorkmap/map.jpg [Yorktown
    map]

Art and Music

http://americanrevolution.org/artmain.html
http://www.contemplator.com/folk/johnny.html

Flags

http://americanrevolution.org/flags2.html
http://www.ushistory.org/betsy/index.html
http://www.walika.com/sr/flags/fedflags1.htm

Other Selected Sites

http://odur.let.rug.nl/~usa/D/1751-1775/bostonmassacre/prest.htm [Boston
    Massacre]
http://douglass.speech.nwu.edu/hanc_a49.htm [Boston Massacre]
http://www.ukans.edu/carrie/docs/texts/bostanon.html [Boston Massacre]
http://www.jmu.edu/madison/wheatley/ [Phyllis Wheatley]
http://www.johnlocke.org/whowasjl.html [John Locke]
http://www.loc.gov/exhibits/british/brit-2.html [British-American tensions]
http://www.si.umich.edu/spies/ [Spy letters]
http://memory.loc.gov/ammem/gwhtml/ [G. Washington Papers at the Library of
    Congress]

Index